Richard Baabereyir Bertino

The Overcomer in Christ

Richard Baabereyir Bertino

The Overcomer in Christ

The Overcomer in Christ

Blessed Hope Publishing

Cover image: www.ingimage.com

Publisher:
Blessed Hope Publishing
is a trademark of
International Book Market Service Ltd., member of OmniScriptum Publishing Group
17 Meldrum Street, Beau Bassin 71504, Mauritius

Printed at: see last page
ISBN: 978-620-2-47794-9

DEDICATION

To God Almighty and my daughter Irenia Yuor Bertino and the entire Bertino family.

ACKNOWLEDGEMENT

My first gratitude goes to the Almighty God for not only the opportunity, but also the guidance and wisdom to go through the writing of this manuscript. I also want to give profound thanks to Elder Amoh Emmanel, Mr. Nana Kyere Sacrifice, Mr. Matthew Donkor, Nana Adakwah Joseph, and Mr. Adu-Gyamfi Paul (King Brutus) for their immense contribution to this success. I cannot afford to overlook the outstanding contribution of Miss Priscilla Opoku for type setting this manuscript.

PREFACE

Grace be unto you, the reader, and peace profound from the Omnipresent Power of God within your consciousness, and within which you abide, now and forever, Amen.

This book is published for solely spiritual guidance. It is a special spiritual warfare treatise set forth to propagate the practical process of "Overcomer's victory over diverse manipulations of all the power of darkness. To this extent, I am fully prepared, by the spirit of God to expose some of the enslavement perpetrate in the world of man by the powers of darkness and their human agents.

I am confident that, this work will surely contribute to bring you closer to the supreme power of the Almighty God, and help in its own way to place you above the devil. I am sincerely indebted to all my Pastor Friends, Associates and Church members who have encouraged me through the grace of God to come out with this book. I sincerely believe that, you will be blessed and lifted.

Let the victory of God be the portion of all those who will faithfully read this book in total submission to our Lord Jesus Christ. Now, the Spirit of God has brought another opportunity of spiritual exposition to YOU, wishing the reader limitless victory in the field of spiritual battle. Amen.

PART 1
The Overcomer

Introduction

This is a book with a difference. It is not one of those books that will entertain you or give you knowledge for knowledge's sake. It is a practical, down-to-earth and simple book that will plant your feet on a rocky foundation as you continue your pilgrim journey through Christ our Lord.
It is the duty of ministers of the gospel to develop the saints and edify them. There are preachers who only succeed at arousing the emotions of believers and making them to feel that, they are victorious when they do not know what it takes to overcome. A lot of believers have been disappointed after they have been assured of victory by so-called 'faith preachers'. Being an overcomer in the real sense of the word is more than practicing the principles of possibility thinking. Instead of just asking you to believe that victory is yours no matter what you do, I am going to be sincere with you by exposing you to Biblical guidelines on how to be an overcomer. I have decided to lay line upon line and dictum upon dictum in order to help all those who will read this book to discover what the 'Overcoming life' is all about.

BIBLICAL PERSPECTIVE

What does the Bible say about the overcomers? What does it take to live the victorious Christian life? How can a believer become an overcomer and keep on living the overcoming life? What are the benefits of overcoming? What are the dangers of just running ahead in one's Christian life without overcoming? These are, among others, the germane questions that agitate the minds of all earnest Bible-believing Christians.

The word of God is very clear on what it means to be an overcomer. People have various views and ideas about the overcomer, and often times, people think that an ignorant believer who don't know how tense the battle is, raises up his/her shoulders and walks about just confessing "I am a child of the king"; "I am an overcomer" etc. is an overcomer. Whenever they see a church member who puts up a bold countenance, looking like a lion, they quickly conclude that, he is an overcomer. Such people are mistaken; they do not know that there are people who look like lions outwardly but are very weak internally. Again, there are people who do not even know the Lord Jesus, and yet they are seen walking up and down bragging that they are overcomers. Such people are not overcomers. Then, there are those whom the devil have left alone because he knows that they are already in his mesh, and for that matter, such people do not experience any trial or temptation. Life is just a bed of roses for such people. The devil knows that, he does not need to trouble them because they are already in his cage.

IGNORANCE ABOUT OVERCOMER'S LIFE IN GOD

A lot of people do not really know what it takes to overcome. There are those who go about saying that, they are overcomers because they had escaped death during a ghastly accident. Others claim of being overcomers because they have not fallen sick for the past one year and over. There are others who go about rejoicing, singing, and confessing that, they are overcomers when they do not know anything about the Christian life. This group of people nursed false hopes concerning going to heaven. They go about saying "We are overcomers", "we belong to the Victorious Christians' Society in my church", when they are only religious. They do not know that, the overcoming life is beyond the reach of religious people.

Not all, there are people who say that, they are born again but go about behaving rudely in an attempt to show others that they are overcomers. Instead of such one to own up to his lack of morals, he/she tries to explain indecent behaviour away by saying: "I am an overcomer", "I will not bow down before anybody". He even tells the Director or the Manager of his place of work, "I am a child of God", "I am a king" and "Nobody can call me a messenger here". People may begin to fear him because he is impudent. Such a person may forget that, he is being feared because of his/her use of audacious face, but not because of any demonstration of Christian virtue. He is deceived into believing that, he is an overcomer when he is only carnal, loud-mouthed and proud. The question we should ask such a person is: Is he supposed to overcome human beings or spiritual forces? Some people have been misled through so-called teachings on the dynamics of faith. After listening to faith messages, they go about claiming what does not belong to them by faith. They might go around saying: "I need this and that now. In the name of Jesus I claim it; it is my right". And because people respond to their impudent behaviour, thinking that they are either mentally upset, or they are babes in spiritual things, they continue to brag. They tell all whom they come in contact with, "I am an overcomer. I get whatever I desire. I don't take 'No' for an answer. I just command people and they give me whatever I ask for". Thus, he becomes deceived.

It is necessary that we know what it means to be an overcomer, so we don't go on deceiving ourselves like many have done in the past. We need to know what the Bible says in order to avoid deceiving others or being deceived by others.

None, whose life is filled with anger, bitterness, pride, evil habits, and the lust of the flesh shout, open his mouth to say that he is an overcomer. Those who tell lies and those who are covetous should not conclude that they are overcomers because of their ability to get anything they desire. There are men who force themselves on innocent Christian ladies in the name of being overcomers. Whenever they come across single ladies they just open their mouths and say "Thus saith the Lord. You must marry me. You can pray, but if you disobey the Lord, you will not get to heaven. Don't ever think that I am interested in marrying you I have come to you because the Lord compelled me to do so. If you don't marry me, you are lost forever. Nobody ever disobeys the Lord and gets to heaven". The unmarried sister might become fearful and answer in the affirmative. The misguided man may go about telling other church members: "I am more than conqueror, my word carries weight. Whenever I talk, my word is the word of a king. Any woman I make a proposal to must agree. The devil is under my feet. I reign in life".

SCRIPTURAL TEACHING OF OVERCOMERS

In view of the widespread misunderstanding and false notions on the overcome life, it is necessary that we closely examine the uniform teaching of Scripture on this subject in order to come out of error and stand on a solid foundation. Numbers (13:30) tells us of a people who knew what to overcome, "And Caleb stilled the people before Moses, and said, Let us go up at once, and possess it; for we are well able to overcome it". From that passage, you can see very clearly that overcoming goes hand in hand with warfare.

Children of Israel who were coming from Egypt needed to dispossess the inhabitants of Canaan of their land. They needed to overcome the Canaanites, drive them out and then become the owners of the territory.

It is very clear from that passage that overcoming means driving away the occupants of a particular territory, and possessing the territory. The territory may be your heart. It is possible that your heart has been occupied by a stranger. You can only lay claim to being an overcomer if you have driven the devil away from your heart and you have enthroned the Lord there. You are only an overcomer when you have banished evil passions, ungodly habits and the lust of the flesh from your heart as well as all the five abnormal faculty of the mind (five perversions/propensities), which are Lust, Anger, Greed, Vanity, and Attachment to mundane things, and you have had it filled with holiness, virtues and the peace of God which passes all understanding. Remember that the scripture says "He that commmitteth sin is of devil: for the devil sinneth from the beginning."

Again, (Numbers 22: 11) reads "Behold, there is a people come out of Egypt, which covereth the face of the earth: come now, curse me them; peradventure I shall be able to overcome them, and drive them out". Again the Bible is very clear here about overcoming. These words came from the lips of Balak. He was talking to Balaam concerning the children of Israel. His purpose was to overcome the children of Israel, to drive every one of them out. If he drove half of them away, he would not accept that he had overcome. If he drove them away from a part of the territory and they occupied a small portion of the territory, he would not agree that he had overcome. He would only say that he had overcome if he succeeded at driving every Israelite away.

Besides, you cannot say that you have overcome until you can look at the territory of your heart, the territory of your family, or the territory of your business without finding any enemy or stranger there. It is only when there is no infiltrator or enemy all around your environment that you can say that you are an overcomer. If you only succeed in driving the enemy away from your business, but he is actively busy perpetrating all kinds of atrocities in your family, you have not overcome yet.

There is nothing like partial victory. You are either an overcomer or you are defeated. You are not an overcomer until you succeed in driving the enemy away completely. If you succeed in driving the enemy away outwardly, but you are smarting internally, you are under the dominion of the devil. Also, you are not an overcomer if you are only able to drive him away from infesting your life with sicknesses. Nor is that all, you are not overcoming if you are holy and healthy, but the enemy is having it roads into your family. If the enemy is occupying the territory of your family or your business but has been driven away from your heart, you are yet to be an overcomer. In the fourth and fifth chapters of the book of judges, much light is thrown on what it means to be an overcomer. The children of Israel had been under the dominion of Canaanites for twenty years. They had suffered defeat and oppression from the hands of Jabin the king of Canaan, and Sisera, the captain of his host. The children of Israel called upon the name of the Lord, and the Lord remembered them. The Bible says "And the LORD discomfited Sisera, and all his chariots, and all his host, with the edge of the sword before Barak; so that Sisera lighted down off his chariot, and fled away on his feet. But Barak pursued after the chariots, and after the host, unto Harosheth of the Gentiles: and all the host of Sisera fell upon the edge of the sword; and there was not a man left" (Judges 4: 15, 16). God gave the children of Israel victory over the Canaanites. Sisera was killed; Jabin the king of Canaan was subdued and destroyed, and the children of Israel had complete victory over their enemies.

Then Deborah and Barak sang a song of victory unto the Lord.
"Awake, Awake, Deborah: awake awake, utter a song: arise, Barak, and lead thy captivity captive, thou son of Abinoam" (Judges 5:12). This verse of scriptures gives us a deep insight into what happens when one has overcome. If you are an overcomer, there will be a song on your lips and there will be "Unspeakable joy full of glory" down deep within your heart. So, if there is sorrow in your heart, if you are discouraged or downcast, you cannot claim to have possessed full victory yet. Your joy can not be full until you have possessed your possession. In view of this the Bible warned us to "….. Put on the whole armour of God that ye may be able to stand against the wiles of the devil." (Ephesians 6: 11)

THE OVERCOMER'S ROLE

More light is thrown on what it means to be an overcomer in (1 John 5:4.) "For whatsoever is born of God overcometh the world: and this is the victory that overcometh the world, even our faith". You need to be born of God in crier to overcome the devil. Verse five reads: "Who is he that overcometh the world, but he that believeth that Jesus is the Son of God?" Again in (1 John 4:4) we were told "Ye are of God, little children, and have overcome them: because greater is he that is in you, than he that is in the world". We do not overcome because we bear Christian names. Neither do we overcome because we attend a good Church. We overcome because Jesus, the Greater One, lives within our hearts. (1John 2:13-14) reads; "I write unto you, fathers, because ye have known him that is from the beginning. I write unto you, young men, because ye have overcome the wicked one. I write unto you, little children, because ye have known the Father, I have written unto you, fathers, because ye have known him that is from the beginning, I have written unto you, young men, because ye are strong, and the word of God abideth in you, and ye have overcome the wicked ones". Here the Bible tells us about the possibility of overcoming the wicked one, There are people who think that, the overcoming life is only an ideal spiritual state and that it is unrealizable, That is not so. The Bible tells us that we can overcome.

How then, can we overcome the wicked one? We must be steadfast and unyielding whenever the devil wages war on us, If the devil comes with symptoms of sicknesses you should not give up and say "I am so sick, the devil is going to kill me"; You should reject the devil's lies and parry off his fiery darts by using the shield of faith, If the devil comes with discouragement and despair, do not start weeping and saying 'There is no hope anymore I might as well commit suicide". You will overcome the wicked by encouraging yourself in the Lord and standing on the unfailing promises of God. If the wicked one comes against you with temptations, if you are a real overcomer, you will not say. "There is neither brother nor sister here (Nobody will know) if I commit sin secretly", rather, your testimony will be "It is written: Whosoever is born of God sinneth not. I am not going to commit sin", this is how to overcome the wicked one.

HOW TO OVERCOMING THE ENEMY

In Bible days, whenever an army goes to the territory of their enemy to wage war against them, it is usually the men in the enemy territory who will come with spears; swords and arrows against them. Whenever the invading army conquers they usually take the men, the children and the women in the captured territory as hostages and captives. They generally lead all captives out of the captured territory into their own land. You can only be said to be an overcomer when you are to go to the territory of the enemy, wage war against the devil and all his cohorts, and emerge victorious.

You are an overcomer if you are able to take authority over Satan and devil spirits and triumph over them. It is when you have succeeded in putting the devil and his lieutenants under your feet that you can lead those who have been under his authority into the kingdom of God. That is what it means to be an overcomer in the real sense of the word. Psalm (68:18) says: "Thou hast ascended on high, thou hast led captivity captive: thou hast received gifts for men; yea, for the rebellious also, that the LORD God might dwell among them". This scripture throws more light on the Biblical perspective on who an overcomer is. It was customary, those days for those who have overcome in a battle to come home with war booties as gifts for those who remained behind. What is the spiritual implication of that practice? When we go to the territory of the enemy to wage war against him, as soldiers of Christ, we go in the strength of the Lord and our faith makes us to ascend up on high. Elevated to heavenly places in Christ Jesus, we begin to shoot arrows at the enemy until he is completely vanquished and until we are completely victorious, As Satan and his cohorts are defeated, and they begin to flee. As they flee, we run after them until they are rounded up. We take them captive and we make an open show of them by triumphing over them. Immediately they are defeated, we enter shoulder high into the domain of the enemy and take all the precious things there. We take all these booties into our territory in order to present them as gifts to those who are waiting for us at home. In that wise, we are not only trying to be overcomer, we are also helping others to overcome. We are not just struggling to overcome the devil; we are so victorious that we are able to help other believers at the valley of defeat to come up to the mountain top of victory.

It is when this has happened that you can actually be said to have overcome in your Christian life. You are an overcomer if you can go to the enemy's territory to fight and come back a victor rather than a victim. Those who are afraid of warfare are not overcomers. Believers who are defeated in battle and those who lose their spiritual power and Christian virtues each time the enemy comes against them, are not overcomers. But if while you are on the battlefield your faith increases, your prayer life become dynamic and your consecration and commitment get deeper, you are an overcomer in the real sense of the word. If you are an overcomer, your strength should be renewed, your power should be increased and the gifts of the spirit should be multiplied in your life whenever you are on the battlefield. You are not only expected to be victorious', you are supposed to be so charged with the Spirits power that you will begin to lay hands on the sick. Deliver the oppressed and lead sinners into the kingdom of God.

Anyone who is defeated at the time of temptation, those who are living in sin, and those who are either running away from spiritual warfare or running away from persecution, are not overcomers. Those who give testimonies saying "I am saved, I am sanctified, I am baptised in the Holy Ghost" but begin to weep whenever there is a little problem in the home, are not overcomers. Those who always run away from the neighbourhood whenever there is a problem instead of defeating the enemy in the strength of the Lord are not overcomers. However, there are soo many ways and aspects of which Christians could overcome Satan, but few are treated below.

OVERCOMING THROUGH THE WORD

Another important step to be taken in order to overcome the wicked one is to study, read and meditate on the word of God, The Bible says: "Let the word of Christ dwell in you richly in all wisdom; teaching and admonishing one another in psalms and hymns and spiritual songs, singing with grace in your hearts to the Lord" (Colossians 3:16), You must allow the word of God to abide in you if you want to be an overcomer, Those who once believed the doctrine of sanctification, but now go about saying that, they are confused concerning the definitive nature of the doctrine, are not overcomers. If you are an overcomer you will constantly stand on the truth. Also, if you are an overcomer, the word of God will remain in your heart in spite of the changing circumstances of life. The word of God will abide in you and dwell richly in you at the time of trial, when you are sorrowful or when you are joyful, if you are an overcomer. Those who abandon the word of God at the time of adversity or because of temporary success are not overcomers.

Hence, Overcomers are usually full of words of faith and victory when others around them are weak, sickly and discouraged. An overcomer lays up God's word richly in his heart even when unbelief and backsliding are the order of the day. An overcomer is generally strong because God's word gives strength. If you want to know what it means to be a spiritual giant, all you need to do is to examine the lives of those whose hearts are filled with the word of God. The Bible says: "For out of the abundance of the heart the mouth speaketh" (Matthew 12:34). When you see a man who always stands on *"It is written"* you have seen an overcomer. You cannot be an overcomer unless you dig deeper into God's word.

OVERCOMING THROUGH TALK(S)

Talk is one of the numerous ways of communication to one another and God (Our creator) and for that matter it is very essential in one's Christian life. There are two main types of talks: — being good or evil. The good one leads a man into his creator in heaven whiles the later gives condemnation. The Bible has warned us in so many ways about how believers should avoid problems for themselves. The scripture says in Proverbs (21:23) that, "Whoso keepeth his mouth and his tongue keepeth his soul from troubles"; and (Ecclesiastes 5:2) also says; "Be not rash with thy mouth, and let not thy thine heart be hasty to utter any thing before God: for God is in heaven and thou upon earth: therefore let thy words be few."
However, Proverbs (10:14) also said: "The wise lay up knowledge: but the mouth of the foolish is near destruction." Why? Because the Bible admonished that; "I tell you, on the day of judgment people will give account for every careless word they speak" (Matthew 12:36). Proverbs (13:3) also said "He that keepeth his mouth keepeth his life; but he that openeth wide his lips shall have destruction" It also said that: "In the multitude of words there wanteth not sin: but he that restraineth his lips is wise" (Proverbs 10:19). Remember that, it is only the thinkable people that should inherit the Kingdom of God but not the fools nor the wise: - when a fool do not talk, he/she is seen and therefore deemed as a wise; "Even a fool, when

he holdeth his peace, is counted wise: and he that shutteth his lips is esteemed a man of understanding," (Proverbs17:28). This tells us that less talk is wealthy enough to commit a fool as wise. Anyone who speaks more is not overcomer because evil shall not depart from his or her mouth always. In Matthew (5:37), the scripture tells us that; "But let your communication be Yea, yea; Nay, nay: for whatsoever is more than these cometh of evil." Be informed that overcomer's life is far advanced of being a religious. A religious person could be a canal being but not a spiritual being. It takes the life of righteousness leading to holiness and perfection to become an overcomer, and the hull mark for such deals with taming the tongue of one self as stipulated in (James 2: 26); " if any man among you seem to be a religious, and bridleth not his tongue, but deceiveth his own heart, this man's religion is vain." This means that even if a religious person should control his/her tongue how much more is an overcomer! His/her is the one who should control the tongue more than necessary. There are some people who claim to be wise, because they are out spoken, without knowing that the more you talk the more you sin and sinners are not partakers in God's kingdom. The Bible says "But your iniquities have separated between you and your God, and your sins have hid his face from you, that he will not hear" (Isaiah 59:2) and ".....we all have fall short in God's glory" (Romans 3: 23). Besides, anyone who talks much is trapped by his/ her own words: "thou art snared with the words of thy mouth, thou art taken with the words of thy mouth......" Proverbs 6:2) leading him/her to hell. Often than not, such people just airing their words without subjecting it to critical thinking, deep thought and understanding. The Bible says "A fool hath on delight in understanding, but that his heart may discover itself" Proverbs 18:2). Be informed that as a believers, we shall be quick to hear, slow to speak and slow to anger, for this is what the scripture admonished us to do; "Know this, my beloved brothers: let every person be quick to hear, slow to speak, slow to anger; (James 1:19). Surprisingly, many believers do not know that, a fool is much better than he who is hasty in speaking, because there is more hope for a fool than such person, "Seest thou a man that is hasty in his words? there is more hope of a fool than of him" (Proverbs 29:20). Moreover, remember that 'Hope' leads to 'Faith', because with accordance to the scripture in Hebrews (11:1); "Now faith is substance of things hoped for, the evidence of things not seen". Therefore the basis of faith is hope, and if a fool has more hope than a talkative (hasty speaking person) then where lays the faith of such believer? Without faith, it is impossible to pleased him:

for he that cometh to God must believer that he is, and that he is a rewarder of them that diligently seek him (Hebrews 11:6). This verse stipulates that, faithless people cannot ascertain to attain a faith by hope that 'God Exist' and acknowledge him as such, of which make them unbelievers to the body of Christ. Further, such person becomes an enemy to Christ because his/her religion is impure. The person has defiled himself herself before God and has corrupted others by vain talks. He/she could not provide protection of their selves and others which is a core responsibility and duty for Christians. The Bible admonished us that, "Pure religion and undefiled before God and the Father is this, to visit the fatherless and widows in their affection, and to keep himself unspotted from the world" (James 1:27); and "Let no corrupt communication proceed out of your mouth, but that which is good to the use of edifying, that it may minister grace unto the hearers" (Ephesians 4:29).

Finally, an overcomer is the one who con tamed the tongue, for that has checked the total body to perfection as an accession of James (3:6); "And the tongue is a fire, a world of iniquity: so is the tongue among our members, that it defileth the whole body, and setteth on fire the course of nature:, and it is set on fire of hell. Jesus said to us in Matthew (12:36), "But I say unto you, That every idle word that men shall speak, they shall give account thereof in the day of judgment." So brethren in Christ let us watch our tongue always. In conclusion of this section, be serious about what you say always because your talks are a standard for live. The bible tells us that he who checks or controls his tongue has putting his whole body in check which pleases the Lord God we served, "For in many things we offend all. If any man offend not in word, the same is a perfect man, and able also to bridle the whole body" (James 3:2) Amen.

OVERCOMING THROUGH THOUGHT

Thought projection is a very confidential aspect of subtle manipulations of powers of darkness against people generally, but I would like to limit myself to manipulations against Christians. The Bible tells us that: "Every day they wrest my words: all their thoughts are against me for evil" (Psalm 56:5). Thought projection is an advanced psychic process in occult operations by which a person or persons are induced or impelled by psychic entities and their higher agents into some repugnant thought. In other words, this is a process of projecting certain thought to a person or persons against God's Will. Different thoughts for sense gratification, or vain thoughts, are always in motion against believers. When the spirits carrying such thoughts strike a person, the mind will be filled from time to time with thoughts bereft of spiritual potency. The stroked person will begin to gratify himself/herself with vain thoughts that impel him/her to raise standards above his/her real self, which gradually leads the person to zero point. The scripture tells us that: "this I say therefore, and testify in the lord, that ye henceforth walk not as other Gentiles walk, in vanity of their mind" (Ephesians 4:17). These people may be quickened to manifest with such thoughts in actions through homogenous attraction. For example, there are occasions in which one may be singing a song in mind but someone around begins to openly sing the very song abruptly. A situation like this is a homogenous attraction thought. It is partial evidence of the fact that thoughts can be transferred from one mind to another with or without physical contact. It can be transferred from one person to another in a subconscious level not only when someone is around you, but regardless of one's distance to another. Thus an intensified thought within the mind of a man in Ghana can be received via homogenous attraction even by a man in say USA or other distant area. Be informed that, the Bible says: "Casting down imaginations, and every high thing that exalteth itself against the knowledge of God, and bringing into captivity every thought to the obedience of Christ" (2 Corinthians 10:5). This Bible verse clearly shows that there is a source of thought that is not of God but of evil one which is Satan and his cohorts. Remember also that in (2 chronicles 18: 19-22), it was the spirit of devil that stepped forward and said to Lord "I will deceive him". How will that come true? The verse 21 says… "The spirit replied, "I will go and make will Ahab's prophets tells lies". Analytically, 'to deceive' oneself comes in a form of speech/ talk as the Bible has declared in the verse above 'tells lies', while the opponent or the receiver will adhered to such thought(s). Here, the prophets had the thought of the spirit- Satan; — 'they all lied to the King Ahab' in verse 22, ("This is what happened. The Lord has made these prophets of yours lie to you."). The manipulation can be done by Satan himself or other millions of his cohorts, directly or indirectly at different places. Be informed that, Satan as an entity could direct project himself occasionally to fight or manipulate a person specifically. Such people are true believers that are identified by Satan himself to be perfectly situated on the path of righteousness. As a matter of truth, without the power of almighty God, the intensity of the direct projection of Satan against a person can finished such one within a second. Even in the Holy Scripture, there are such direct projections against great and righteous men of God. Briefly, let us consider these characters in the Bible. "And he shewed me Joshua the high priest standing before the angel of the LORD, and Satan standing at his right hand to resist him. And the LORD said unto Satan, the LORD rebuke thee, O Satan, even the LORD that hath chosen Jerusalem rebuke thee…." (Zachariah3:1-2). This quotation shows an incident of direct projection of the entity Satan, who tried to 'resist' Joshua. He knew that, Joshua being the high priest of God, if could be manipulated, then there will be cut off the free flow of God power from him; for the people of God live to in darkness and ignorance of God's facts. He knew that to bet Joshua means being held the whole people of God in captivity for his kingdom, so he directly appeared to resist him. Nevertheless, the Lord God himself immediately rebuked Satan and banished him from the high priest Joshua. More so, on the account of Job, the Scripture says: "….was perfect and upright, and one that feared God, and eschewed evil." He was also "the greatest of all the men of the east" (Job 1:1-3). Satan being known all these credentials of job, he decided to destroy him by asking God to allow him (Satan) to tempt His faithful servant Job. God allowed him to try his best to tempt Job, but not his life. The scripture says: "So went Satan forth from the presence of the LORD, and smote He went on Job with sore boils from the sole of his foot unto his crown. And he took him a potsherd to scrape himself withal; and he sat down among the ashes" (Job 2:7-8). He tempted Job directly on all aspects of his life style. However, Jesus was tempted directly by Satan severally "Then saith Jesus unto him, Get thee hence Satan…Then the devil leaveth him…" (Matthew 4:10-11). Hence, on a conscious level; this is used for subtle psychic manipulations. In other words, an advanced occult psychic forces process can be used to manipulate the thought of people, and in consequence subject such people to Maya (zero/ illusion point), through the final manipulation of such thoughts in their actions. In the advanced battle of powers of darkness against believers, different categories of spirits are projected in motion by Elam (An angel of Satan; transformed as a minister of Jesus Christ in Astral and Terrestrial realms of spirit) in the city of Retz of the Venus planet, to the Christians on the earth planet at every Sunday by 3:00am. He is responsible for all manipulations against Christians in pretext or disguise as an angel of light or 'wolf in a sheep's clothe.' Nevertheless, the Bible admonished that: "And no marvel; for Satan himself is transformed into an angel of light" (2 Corinthians 11:14). These spirits are evoked by Elam are responsible for subjecting human agents on earth, who use them to manipulate believers in diverse ways. Nevertheless, if you are strong daily in the power of Almighty God, then Satan himself will be under your feet: "and the God of peace shall bruise Satan under your feet…" but this promise awaits the overcomers alone, remember that and live overcoming life. Amen.

OVERCOME THROUGH FOOD

In different parts of the world, human beings are mysteriously transformed into animals, whilst the flesh of such animals is in turn used to enslave people via divers' elements of darkness. An element of darkness is not a spirit being (demon), but it is something constructed by demons for the purpose of enslaving people through what they eat. Apart from food, however, an element of darkness can still be planted in one's body through sexual act, smoking, snuffing and other mundane things. The moment you eat a human flesh in the form of animal meat, the forces of darkness will use same to contaminate and dominate your life. Further, be informed that, to a greater extent unknown to most of you readers, what you eat in both spiritual (dreams) and physical can go a long way to determine the level of your spiritual power. In physical world, scientific studies prove that, we gain nutrients from the food we eat; which goes down to give tripartite functions as energy, growth and protection sources to our bodies. Moreover, these three main nutrients that functions in our bodies, aid in building the Body's Cells of which builds the Body Tissues for an advancement buildering of our Organs; which collectively forms the Body's Personality– Body and Spirit. Remember that, the Bible tells as in (1Corinthains15:44-46) that, "It is sown a natural body; it is raised a spiritual body. There is a natural body, and there is a spiritual body. Howbeit that was not first which is spiritual, but that which is natural; and afterward that which is spiritual. Therefore the food we eat which builds our body physically, which translates into the state of our Spiritual Being. In clear terms, the food we eat has direct grossing effect on our Spirit Being. The nutrients from the food we eat builds our bodies which facilitate the individuals to behave in a certain way; which provides habit, and in turn fashioned attitude for one's behaviour to be seen. This is a major reason why sometimes Physicians/ Medical Practitioners diagnosed people and asked them to eat or top eating some type (s) of food, if found that the problem associated with the person is from diet. There are some cases whereby people take in food substance (s) and feel abnormal with the body there after or their attitude changed as an anticipated from allergies (antipathies). What happened or is the causer? It is due to the gross material elements made up the food, and it is true that vibration of gross element is coarse in essence. Nevertheless, eating of food is a process of adding an external material element to the already existing naturally made material element of the body. Base on this, the coarse vibration of food you took dominates that of your naturally made body for some time. This explains why sometimes you feel bad after eating or unusual sensation. Notwithstanding, when this happened, the intensity of the minute (microscopic) subtle energy of the human body is naturally lowered to the extent that, the Spirit of God working through the human spirit, cannot exert the vigorous force in the physical system of reality required for the protection of the body against spiritual attacks especially in dream state. Contrastingly, if being awaits for not less than three hours of eating before sleeping, the negative vibration of the food taken will totally dissolved, thus enhancing the potency of human spirit to dominate the propensity of the body. It is through this process that the Spirit of God will transcend you holistically by Spirit, Soul and Body, to co-ordinate your dream experienced and protect your life against any spiritual attack mostly at sleep stage. Nevertheless, if you use such three hour after taken food for say, watching film or a thing that gratified material senses or talks that is devoid of glory of God, by so doing, you are setting up a negative fabric of darkness in motion against yourself of which demons/ evil spirits can still dominate you in dreams.

Also, startlingly, many believers as well as some great men of God are ignorant of the fact that, what they eat can seriously determine their spiritual level of power. It could be recalled that some great Prophets of old times (Olden days), as well as Jesus Christ himself were given specific instructions by the Spirit of God on the kind of food to be eaten while on earth, even before their birth. Many people are unaware that, what Jesus Christ ate whiles on earth as a revelation directive by the Holy Spirit before his birth. Hitherto, it is evident that, most believers are not even aware that what they eat can either uplift or degrade their spiritual powers (Spiritual Growth), depending on the nature of the food they eat. Moreover, the scripture says, Jesus Christ accounted for eaten ...... "Therefore the Lord Himself shall give you a sign: Behold, a virgin shall conceive, and bear a son, and shall call his name Immanuel. Butter and honey shall he eat, that he know to refuse the evil, and choose the good" (Isaiah 7: 14-15). When you recognise the ultimate spiritual essence of why Jesus ate "honey ad butter" on earth, you will begin to comprehend that, what you eat can either uplift or degrade your consciousness, and power. Jesus is the lord of the universe, but when He was on earth as human to save us, He needed to operate and uphold higher spiritual principles, so as to completely overcome all the devices of the Prince of Darkness. One of such principles is the type of food He ate. Why did Jesus eat honey and butter? According to the scripture…….. "So that He may know to refuse the evil, and choose good." The phrase "to refuse the evil" implicated to do with victory. If I refuse evil, then I have overcome evil. In other words, Christ ate honey and butter to enable Him overcome evil— refuse the evil and choose good. He set for Himself this principle before manifested physically. He did not eat honey and butter for handsomeness or to accumulate material wealth, but solely "that He may know to refuse evil, and choose good". Truly certain food can assist you to overcome devil manipulations and power. This is very vital, Sampson had such Biblical Principle before his birth, but he failed and had his doomed, because he did not succumbed to what the angle said before his birth through his parents. The scripture says in (Judges 13:4), "Now therefore beware, I pray thee, and drink not wine nor strong drink, and eat not any unclean thing". The Judges chapter (14:9) tells us that: Samson ate unclean food which was one of his failure causer "……and he took thereof in his hands and went on eating and came to his father and mother, and he, and he gave them, and they did eat: but he told not them the he had taken the honey out of the carcase of the loin". Nowadays, many children of God are weak in both physical and spiritual because they pay no or little attention to the food they eat. The fact is that, sin came to this world through food (Genesis. 3:6) "…. she took of the fruit thereof, and did eat, and gave also unto her husband with her; and he did eat". As believer, be informed as I said early on that major element of darkness for enslavement is food that is why Satan (The Snake) coaxed them through food. So beloved in Christ, Never compromised with food in your life. An Apostle Paul also warned believers about how we eat, because he knew the consequences of eating and its effects on children of God in both spiritual and physical reams. In Romans (14: 21), he said; "it is good neither to eat flesh, nor drink wine, nor any thing whereby thy brother stumbleth, or is offended ,or is made weak". This accession tells us that, one may be weaken through food. He also said in (1Corinthians11:29-30)

“For he that eateth and drinketh unworthily, eateth and drinketh damnation to himself…” and “For this cause many are weak and sickly among you, and many sleep.” It also implies that, many of us are now weaken in both physical and spiritual through how we eat, and we eat to bring judgement (damnation) as well as sickness upon ourselves. Be informed that, there are two levels of Spiritual Science: being Primary level and Higher Platform Level. A person operating on Primary level could eat all things– all sorts of food, but on the Higher Platform Level, one has to eat only those things (Food) that could enable him/her maintain the highest vibrations of spiritual powers. This is an evident in the lives of our Lord Jesus Christ, John the Baptist, and some great old prophets which operated such higher platform, and it is not good for such one to eat all things in the thought that he/she could use prayer to sanctify them. John the Baptist is one of the great beings of the highest spiritual consciousness. Consequently, when he came into the world of man, he ate such things that enabled him maintain the power of the Lord in him. The scripture spoke of him thus: “and the same John had his raiment of camel’s hair, and a leathern girdle about his loins; and his meat was locust and wild honey” (Matthew 3:4). Some of us think that we can eat all sorts of food and still maintain the highest power of God within our consciousness, but that is not the true situation. You may wrongly think also that the case of both Jesus Christ and John the Baptist do not apply to other spiritual men on the higher path of life. Of course, all believers are not on the same level of spiritual powers, but whosoever wants to advance to the highest point of the supreme power of God available for the children of men, must follow the bonafide path of not eating all sorts of food. Furthermore, recalled that Prophet Daniel and other three Jewish – Shadrach, Meshach and Abendenago who refused to eat all sorts of food given to them in the palace of the King of Babylon. They rather requested vegetables from the steward. The scripture says: “Thus Melzar took away the portion of their meat, and the wine that they should drink; and gave them pulse” (Daniel 1:16). The results of these aforementioned four Jewish men action as reported by Bible is: “Now at the end of the days that the king had said he should bring them in, then the prince of the eunuchs brought them in …….. And all matters of wisdom and understanding, that the king enquired of them, he found them ten times better than all the magicians and astrologers that were in all his realm” (Daniel 1:20)

However, from this end, if you still wish to eat all sorts of food, you can do so, but those who are sincerely out to advance on the path of spiritual science and thus live above the devil, must obey the primordial Will of God on the nature of food that man should eat." And God said, Behold, I have given you every herd bearing seed, which is upon the face of all the earth, and every tree, in the which is the fruit of a tree yielding seed; to you it shall be for meat" (Genesis 1:29); Psalm (104:14) says "He causeth the grass to grow for the cattle, and herb for the service of man: that he may bring forth food out of the earth." Now, for your own conviction, eat only fruits once in a day at 6pm, for seven days or beyond, without eaten any other thing at the period. You will discover a new level of Power of Godin you unfold to a greater degree via diverse manifestations. A word is enough to a wise.

It is concluded that, sincerely speaking, food is the major agent of enslavement for power of darkness against the people of this world— earthmen. It was not in vain that Christ himself, our perfect example, ate honey and butter so as to overcome evil and know and do good always —"butter and honey shall he eat, that he may know to refuse the evil and choose good," (Isaiah 7:15).

OVERCOMING THROUGH SLEEP

The planet earth is a region of spiritual battle. The sinners who have strange gods and who serve demons have war in their gates, because they war against their creator. The believers are in warfare against principalities and power of darkness. While Satan ('Sat an' its occult name or Chitanam) and his fallen spirits are fighting against the faithful and the faithless. The earth life is full of battle in all aspects.

In every physical war there must be a war front or battlefield. The same applies to spiritual battle as far as evil powers are concerned. Many people are aware that there is a spiritual war going on in this life, but some are not aware of the major areas declared by the enemy to be the main battlefield. I wish to emphasise that your period of sleep or the sleep state is the war front (Where war is much intensified/ hot) of the manipulations of psychic forces against you. I am not saying that your sleep period is the time you have to consciously fight the spirits of evil, but that is the time the forces of darkness intensify their battle against you. Be informed that, here are 30,000,000.00 centres of psychic and metaphysical powers (powers of darkness) on earth. Each centre serves as a constant meeting point of the spirits of Satan and their human agents on earth. Now, each centre is also responsible for sending out a highly concentrated unit of astral power, in the form of sleep-wave, at every midnight. The waves are launched spiritually worldwide and its projection is on true believers of Christ from 3am-6am daily. These centres are scattered in diverse places such as hilly, forest, occult temples, markets, trees, road junctions, deserts and mountains, to mention but a few. Sleep-waves from the kingdoms of darkness are specifically projected against believers who are prayerful. It is evident that prayer is a major tool in the hand of a believer against the kingdoms of darkness, and the sleep-wave comes from the forces of darkness to counteract against the power of prayer. A prayerful believer is a powerful believer. If you are a prayerful believer, sleep-wave all always visit you. It is the vibration of prayer that enables the sleep –wave to recognise you. Therefore you are vehemently advice to maintain your level of prayer as prayerful being, that is the only way you can remain victor over sleep-wave and all the powers of darkness. Guide yourself with this knowledge: the best time for you to pray is when you feel weak to pray. Please don't forget this!

Notwithstanding, someone under the influence of sleep-wave is spiritually reduced by the forces of darkness, of which a prayerful believer can be reduced to the bearing lowest level of lethargy; so don't be surprised when you found yourself in this situation. At the lowest manipulation reduction level you may find yourself sometimes asleep or sleeping during prayer section(s) to extent that you may be saying all sort of things you ought not to say: - spending several seconds saying vain words, speaking repugnant words. An influence believer on sleep-wave can say "I bind you Jesus" instead of "I bind you Satan" in a prayer section, some may try to be awake by shaken their bodies in prayer section to show an activeness while in reality he/she had slept off; this is a duty of sleep-wave against a believer. Be informed that, if you are under sleep-wave influence, the moment you want to prayer alone or in the midst of others, heavy sleep befallen/ descended on you, which is in continues weaken different units of the power of Godin you to the detriment of your entire spiritual existence. Through this sleep-wave induction, you will discover that, the sleep leaves you the moment the prayer ends. Furthermore, brethren, if you are at the lowest level, you surely need a revival; otherwise you will soon get yourself in a 'hot soup'. Please, fall on able believers to aid you in prayer or deliverance immediately with regardless of your spiritual position. Remember that, God love humble servants and the elect of God can be taken away by Satan; (Matthew 23:11-12) "The greatest among you will the servant. For whoever exalts himself will be humbled, and whoever humbles himself will be exalted." This is the level of life Satan wants us to live with while on earth. Sincerely speaking, you must be disciplined to learn how to be honest and admit your weakness/fault, so that you can be delivered from sleep-wave. As a believer, don't witticism with your prayer life for the Bible said "Arise, cry out in the night: in the beginning of the watches pour thine heart like water before the face of the LORD: lift up thy hands toward him for the life of thy young children, hat faint for hunger in the top of every street". This is because Jesus one said; "Watch and pray that ye enter not into temptation: the spirit indeed is willing, but the flesh is weak."(Matthew 26:41). Note that, in the mode of prayer, God uses a believer as a channel though which his Holy Spirit set in motion against even the supreme flood of the Prince of Darkness; "...... when the enemy shall come in like a flood; the Spirit of the Lord shall lift up a standard against him."(Isaiah: 59:19). Through true worship and warfare prayer, the set-up organisational systems of the kingdoms of darkness are disentangled, and Satan and his cohorts will dislike you, but if you are not prayerful Christian, Satan will surely like you. Be lovers in Christ; recall that, the spirits in charge of sleep-wave activities have no other duty than to fight true believers with full time of their power of sleep, so remember to safeguard yourselves. Please if you have known that you are under sleep-wave influence recite the Fourth Spiritual Decree five times every 12:00 midnight and at 3:00 am for a week and will be delivered by the Omnipotent power of God. Amen!

It is well known in occultism and witchcraft operations that, no esoteric or metaphysical power cannot dominate a person when such a one is not physically asleep, except the person is at zero point (Maya), all the known projected attack against a person , can only subdue him/ her in sleep state. This is why any true follower of our Lord Jesus Christ wishing to always overcomer every demonic attack must strive also to overcome much sleep. More so, it is not in vain that Jesus Christ admonished "Watch and pray that ye enter not into temptation; the spirit indeed is willing, but the flesh is weak." (Matthew 26: 41). Jesus said! ... "Watch and pray", Why! That, you don't enter "into temptation." What happened if you do not watch and pray? The answer is: "You will enter into temptation". Note that our Lord did not say "watch or pray," He said "watch and pray." It implies that both should be done simultaneously, so as to overcome the manipulations of the Price of Darkness.

Indeed, there is NO human being on earth who sleeps for a whole eight hours and beyond within every twenty –four hours who is not actively prone to demonic attack. However, believers who sleep for not six hours and beyond are in better position to overcome demonic manipulations which come through sleep period. For instance, those who subdivided six hours sleep into smaller hours of sleep can never be manipulated by dark forces as far as sleep/dream manipulations are concerned. E.g. Sleeping within six hours which is subdivided as 2hrs, 1hr, 2hrs and 1hr. Notwithstanding, with this, the Bible says:.....“But while men slept, his enemy came and sowed tares among the wheat, and went his way.” (Math. 13:25). This has remembered me of the Bible sorry concerning two prostitutes' women… “And this woman's child died in the night; because she overlaid it. And she arose at midnight, and took my son from beside me, while thine handmaid slept, and laid it in her bosom, and laid her dead child in my bosom.” The above scripture laid hold to the fact that, it is because of the slept (sleeping) that is why her live child was change for the dead one. In view of this, the scripture warned us that; … “Give not sleep to thine eyes, nor slumber to thine eyelids, deliver thyself as a roe from the hand of the hunter, and as a bird from the hand of the flower” (Proverb 6: 4-5).

THE OVERCOMER'S ATTITUDE

The believer must exhibits an attitude of overcomers. The scripture warned us …. “For though we walk in the flesh, we do not war after the flesh: (For the weapons of our warfare are not carnal, but mighty through God to the pulling down of strong holds) Casting down imaginations, and every high thing that exalted itself against the knowledge of God, and bringing into captivity every thought to the obedience of Christ” (2Corinthians 10:3-5). In your relationship with members of your family, church, Pastor(s), and, with God, there are times when the devil will shoot fiery darts at you by bringing up thoughts that will almost sweep you off your feet. A number of thoughts will come into your heart, but you have to resist the devil's suggestions. The devil will shoot arrows at you by telling you that all those who are around you do not love you at all. He will also tell you that your pastor hates you. He will bring diverse kinds of thoughts into your heart in order to defeat you. He will try to make you lose confidence in yourself and in God. He will make you to believe that you cannot do any good thing. He will make you feel that everybody hates you. If you are a Christian woman he will make you feel that your husband has something against you when his heart is full of love and appreciation for you. The devil is the accuser of the brethren. He is notorious for bringing ruinous thoughts into the hearts of God's people. The victorious man overcomes all the imaginations that the devil brings up in his mind and pulls down all satanic strongholds in his life. Those who claim to be saved, sanctified and baptised in the Holy Ghost, but cannot deal with the imaginations that come up in the heart, are not overcomers. There are believers who find it difficult to remain in a church where they are not allowed to manifest self-will and rebellion. As soon as some people discover that they are in a church where there is strict discipline, they begin to think of running away to a place where things are *"lighter"*. Such people are not overcomers. If you run away each time there is a problem, it is an indication that you are not an overcomer. If after you have prayed, you do not seem to get any answer, and then you make up your mind to have nothing again to do with prayer, you are not en overcomer. If you give up because of imaginations just at the point you are to receive the greatest blessing of your life, you are not an overcomer. The Bible says: "If thou faint in the day of adversity, thy strength is small" (Proverbs 24:10). A real overcomer will keep on holding on until victory is won.

If you want to be an overcomer, you must deal with your heart. You must bring all strange voices under subjection, or you must allow the supernatural hands of God to touch your heart so that it will be made holy and pure. Also, you must enthrone the Lord Jesus in your heart by making Him the One who rules and reigns in your life without any rival. You cannot be an overcomer as long as you give half-hearted devotion and loyalty to the Lord. The one who is one leg in the kingdom and another leg in the world cannot be an overcomer. If you have tried to be an overcomer without succeeding, you might have to check up concerning the one who occupies the throne of your heart. More so, you will experience victory if the Lord reign without rival in your heart.

More so, (Proverbs 16: 32) says "He that is slow to anger is better than the mighty; and he that ruleth his spirit than he that taketh a city". Those who go about telling people "In the name of Jesus; I claim your salary. It is mine; thinking that they are mighty", are not overcomers. Such people are only covetous; they are not overcomers. Also, those who can be so angry to the point of destroying things, claiming that they were so angry with the devil that the power of God came mightily upon them, are deceiving themselves. Anger is not a virtue. The believer who rules his spirit and controls his temper when he is under serious provocation is an overcomer indeed. He who is slow to anger as well as he who is gentle and loving is an overcomer. You are only an overcomer if you possess the ability to care for people and serve them rather than bully them despotically.

THE OVERCOMERS MATURITY

An overcomer is someone who has a good measure of maturity. You must be able to control your emotions if you say that you are an overcomer. If you allow your thoughts to run riot, if you allow your mind to be agitated because of certain pressing issues, if you have no control over your mind, you are not an overcomer. If you are a real overcomer you must be able to control your emotions even when bad news is brought to you. Also, you must be able to keep your passions under control.

Some Pentecostals are at a loss concerning what the overcoming life is all about. Although they profess to possess spiritual gifts, they do not know how to rule their spirits. They have forgotten what the Bible says: “And the spirits of the prophet are subject to the prophets. For God is not the author of confusion, but of peace, as in all churches of the saints” (1Corinthians 14:32-33). If you go to certain assemblies you will be shocked when you see all that go on there. It is not uncommon to find misguided individuals who would rise up to speak in tongues when the preacher is still preaching. If such a person is upbraided, he might come up with a statement like “I was so much in the Spirit that I could not control myself”. He is not an overcomer. Those who burst into tongues while the preacher is preaching are not overcomers. An overcomer is one who can rule his spirit.

THE OVERCOMER'S ARMOUR

The Bible tells us in (Ephesians 6: 10-14) how to maintain our victory “Finally, my brethren, be strong in the Lord, and in the power of his might. Put on the whole armour of God that ye may be able to stand against the wiles of the devil. For we wrestle not against flesh and blood, but against principalities, against powers, against the rulers of the darkness of this World, against spiritual wickedness in high places. Wherefore take unto you the whole armour of God that ye may be able to withstand in the evil day, and having done all, to stand. Stand therefore, having your loins girt about with truth, and having on the breastplate of righteousness". Paul the apostle was with the military attire and the weapons of the Roman soldier. He was also familiar with the way the children of Israel armed themselves for battle. He counsels the believer to be fully armed just as the Roman soldier was fully armed. Again, he says that the believer should have his loins girt about with truth. In those days it was customary for the children of Israel to take the skin of animals and write the promises of God on them and put them on as part of their dressing for battle. They believed that the promises of God which they wore as a belt would make them victorious at all times. What Paul the apostle was saying is that we need to wrap our hearts and lives with the word of God in order to overcome.

Paul the Apostle continues in verse 15 "And your feet shod with the preparation of the gospel of peace; Above all, taking the shield of faith, wherewith ye shall be able to quench all the fiery darts of the wicked. And take the helmet of salvation, and the sword of the Spirit, which is the word of God: Praying always with all prayer and supplication in the Spirit, and watching thereunto with all perseverance and supplication for all saints" (Ephesians 6: 15-18). The picture painted by Paul in this passage is the picture of an overcomer. You are expected to overcome in all point and in all things. Partial victory, half-hearted commitment, Luke warmness and haphazard devotion are not acceptable to the Lord. You have to keep your Christian experiences, watch your attitude and maintain a consistent walk with the Lord in order to be an overcomer. It is when you take care of all the minute things that make someone an overcomer, that you will really experience what it takes to be an overcomer. From all that you have read so far I know you now understand what it means and what it takes to be an overcomer. I am sure you are going to obey the Lord God in all that He is going to reveal to you in this book (Amen!)

BENEFITS FOR OVERCOMMERS

What are the benefits of overcoming? There are numerous promises and benefits awaiting the overcomers in the scripture. At this age when the standard has been lowered and adulterated, you must watch your life lest you join the bandwagon of hypocrites. Divorce and remarriage, fornication and adultery, as well as worldly fashion and music have now become rampant in the church. Many professing Christians and ministers are total strangers to the overcoming life. But if you want to be an overcomer you will uphold and live by the word of God wherever you are. You will do well to call to mind the blessed future that awaits the overcomer whenever you are tempted to compromise or sin against God. Some of such benefits are as follows:

- Revelation 2:7 says "He that hath an ear, let him hear what the Spirit saith unto the churches; To him that overcometh will give to eat of the tree of life, which is in the midst of the paradise of God". There are wonderful promises in the word of God for the believer who dares to be an overcomer in the midst of fiery trials and temptations. Untold benefits have been reserved for the overcomer. One of these benefits is that the overcomer will eat the tree of life. This is what Adam and Eve lost because of disobedience, and what mankind has never had access to since the time of the fall. This fruit will be given to overcomers. The future of the overcomer is bright. It is beyond compare.

- "He that hath an ear, let him hear what- the Spirit saith unto the churches: He that overcometh shall not be hurt of the second death" (Revelation 2:11). The greatest benefit to be enjoyed by overcomers is access to heaven. No price is too high to pay if one wants to escape hell. Those who, for one reason or the other, fail to overcome will regret eternally in hell. It is folly to go about saying "It doesn't matter if I cannot overcome". It matters, No matter what you have done for the Lord, all your labour will be in-vain if you fail to overcome. Mere profession cannot make you an overcomer. All that you have suffered would be in vain should you fail to overcome. All the efforts you have put into Christian living and service would have been wasted if you are found wanting at the end of life. All the persecution which you endured would not be remembered, if you miss the mark at the end of your Christian life. If you want to be an overcomer, you must not allow anybody to tamper with the doctrines of the word of God which you have believed. You can travel to any part of the world but you must hold fast to the word of God. You must ensure that your life and conduct are in conformity with the word of God. No matter what other professing Christians are doing you must make up your mind to be a Bible Christian.

- He that hath an ear, let him hear what the spirit saith to the churches; "To him that Overcomth will I give to eat of the hidden manna, and will give him a white stone, and in the stone a new name written which no man knoweth saving he that received it" (Rev. 2:17)

- But that which ye have already hold fast till I come. And he that overcometh, and keepeth my works unto the end, to him I will give power over the nations: and shall he rule them with a rod of iron; as the vessels of a potter shall they be broken to shivers: even as I received of my father. And I will give him the morning star" (Rev. 2: 25-28).

- Revelation 3:5 says "He that overcometh, the same shall be clothed in white raiment; and I will not blot out his name out of the book of life, but I will confess his name before my Father, and before his angels". You must overcome if you want your name to remain in the book of life. Also you must keep on overcoming if you want Jesus Christ to give a testimony of victory and faithfulness concerning you.

- Another promise that has been given by the Lord to all overcoming saints can be found in (Revelation 3:12) "Him that overcometh will make a pillar in the temple of my God, and he shall go no more out: and I will write upon him the name of my God, and the name of the city of my God, which is new Jerusalem, which cometh down out of heaven from my God: and I will write upon him my new name". This means only overcomers will have the authority to bear God's name and live with him perpetually or everlastingly.

- The overcomer is also given another premise in Revelation chapter three verse twenty-one: "To him that overcometh will grant to sit with me in my throne, even as I also overcame, and am set down with my Father in his throne". What a wonderful promise! God has made a wonderful provision for overcomers. It is only overcomers who will experience the indescribable thrill and glory that God has prepared for those who love Him. Jesus is our perfect example. He is the author and finisher of our faith (Heb. 12:2). He demonstrated what it means to overcome when he was on earth. His life and death is an example to all who want to tread the overcomer's path. Jesus wants us to overcome as He overcame.

- Revelation 21:7 says "He that overcometh shall inherit all things; and I will be his god, and he shall be my son".

Finally, Jesus overcame all through the days he spent on earth. He said: "These things have I spoken unto you, that in me ye might have peace. In the world ye shall have tribulation: but be of cheer; I have overcome the world" (John 16: 33). Whether in the wilderness, or amidst hostile religious leaders, he was always victorious. Jesus overcame in the public as well as in His private life. You have been called to overcome as Jesus overcame. Do not make anyone your model, but follow Jesus in all you dealings. If you overcome as He overcame, you will sit with Him on His throne and all other promises stated above are yours forever and ever. Amen

Part 2
How to overcome Temptation

Introduction

The problem of temptation is a common problem to all and sundry. We become more conscious of temptation when we become believers. When someone comes to the Lord in repentance, he /she experiences salvation. The light of God shines within him/her that, the devil becomes unhappy and tries to make a shipwreck of his faith by tempting him. The devil knows that, the believer is on his way to glorious land. He therefore tries to do his best in order to hinder the believer from getting to heaven and from being successful in the Christian race. The strategy employed by the devil entails hurling temptations at the believer in rapid successions and with diabolical intensity until he turns back from following the Lord.

TEMPTATION: WHAT IT IS?

What is temptation? Temptation is an enticement to do evil. You are being tempted anytime you receive a suggestion to do evil. Whenever the devil entices you to do what is contrary to the word of God, you are facing temptation. The Bible says "My son, if sinners entice thee, consent thou not If they say, Come with us, let us lay wait for blood, let us lurk privily for the innocent without cause: We shall find all precious substance, we shall fill our houses with spoil: Cast in thy lot among us; let us all have one purse: My son, walk not thou in the way with them; refrain thy foot from their path" (Proverbs 1:10,11,13-15). From this passage an enticement or an inducement to do what is sinful is what the Bible terms as temptation. The writer of the book of proverbs here describes vividly what temptation is all about. Temptations generally promise pleasure, riches and some benefits that will become yours if you yield to it. The tempter will make you to believe that these benefits, profits, pleasures or some good things will become yours if you yield to temptation. The Spirit of God, speaking through the writer of the Proverbs, counsels the believer to shun such allurements/cajoles and steer clear from the pathway of tempters and temptresses. Although the fact of temptation is an undeniable one yet the believer who chooses to be an overcomer can be victorious in the midst of fierce temptations.

Temptation is not sin; it is yielding to it: — that is sinful. A lot of believers contend with temptations day after day. Some do not just know how to handle temptations. Sad still, a good many zealous believers have been slain by the pebbles of temptation. Both old believers and young Christians are always eager to receive help on how to overcome temptation.

Since our attitude to temptation will determine where we will spend eternity, it is important to get acquainted with proven principles on how to overcome temptations. If present-day believers are exposed to how to win in the battle against sin, we will have more victorious believers, less backsliding and more new converts will be established in the faith. A dynamic army of victorious believers will be the resultant upshot of a sound understanding of the Biblical teaching on how to overcome temptation.

The subjects of victor, over temptations litter the pages of the Bible. The scripture makes it crystal clear that, every believer ought to be victorious in temptation. Victory over temptation is not a sumptuous experience meant for a chosen few, it is for whoever dare put on the whole armour of God. In God's economy, Christian men and women, young believers, adult believers, old timers, ministers, Christian workers and all categories of believers, are supposed to experience and enjoy victory at the time of temptation. The Bible has not only projected the possibility of experiencing victory over temptation, it has also provided necessary guide-lines concerning how to overcome in the battles of life.

THE SOURCE OF TEMPTATION

Knowing the source of temptation is an important factor as far as victory over temptation is concerned. When you recognize the source of the temptations that come your way, you will be able to face it with iron resistance. When your eyes are opened to the fact, that all temptations and enticement to do evil come from a source that hates you, wants to destroy you physically and wants to ruin your spiritual life, you will no longer see temptations as: child's play, rather, you will make up your mind to quash all the fiery darts of the wicked one. No matter how subtle the wicked one is, no matter how sweet and pleasant are his allurements, no matter how sound and convincing are his arguments, do not consensus when he entices you. If you consent, he will draw your soul to hell. In James (1:13-15) says: "Let no man say when he is tempted, I am tempted of God: for God cannot be tempted with evil, neither tempteth he any man: But every man is tempted, when he is drawn, away of his own lust, and enticed. Then when lust hath conceived, it bringeth forth sin: and sin, when it is finished, bringeth forth death". God does not tempt anybody with evil. Whenever a suggestion to do evil comes to you, settle it in your heart that it is not from God but from the devil. There are believers who inadvertently conclude that temptations come from God. This is not true. If you believe in your heart that God is the tempter, you have been deceived into seeing the tempter as someone who loves you. It is the strategy of the devil to keep you ignorant concerning the author and the source of temptation. He will pull a man deeper and deeper into temptation and sin as long as he can keep him ignorant to what is happening to him. The true source of temptation is revealed in (1Chronicles 21: 1) "And Satan stood up against Israel, and provoked David to number Israel". Satan is the tempter. The word 'provoke' is a very powerful word. Have you ever seen a man who provoked another man? A man can be said to have been provoked when his emotions, feelings and desires have been affected negatively. Satan provokes people to do what is evil. He generally provokes people and tries to hurry them up to act instantly. Wherever the devil pushes you and tells you "Thus is your chance, act quickly and do it now", he is luring you into evil. He will not allow you to settle down and reason whether the action he wants you to take is sinful or not. He will convince you about the immediacy of the action he wants you to take, the satisfaction you will derive from it and he will give you a thousand and one reasons why you must act according to his suggestion. Whenever the devil wants to provoke you to do evil he usually makes the temptation sharp, strong and sudden making you unable to reason and rendering your resistance weak and, making you too confused to take any contrary action. That is the strategy of the devil, the tempter.

Matthew chapter four gives us the account of the temptation of Jesus. "Then was Jesus led up of the Spirit into the wilderness to be tempted of the devil" (Matthew

4:1). Here, the identity of the tempter as well as the source of temptation is given to us. We are given a clue on who the tempter is. The Bible here removes the mask from the tempter, the devil, and reveals his true identity. Whenever there is an urge to do evil and a driving passion to do what the Bible forbids takes hold of you, remember that the devil is its source, and quickly renounce all suggestions to act contrary to "thus saith the Lord".

The source of temptation is vividly portrayed in verse three. "And when the tempter came to him, he said, "If thou be the Son of God, command that these stones be made bread". Jesus, at this time, was hungry because he had fasted for forty days and forty-nights. It is legitimate to be hungry; it is also legitimate to eat when one is hungry. But the tempter will tempt you and persuade you to do a legitimate thing in an illegitimate way. He will attempt to lure you into satisfying legitimate appetites in illegitimate ways. He will tell you to use your authority, resources, wealth, personality and identity in a wrong way. The devil will try to convince you to do what is right in a wrongful manner. It was proper for Jesus to break a forty day fast by eating, but it was wrong to use His authority and power in obedience to the suggestion of the devil. So, whenever there is a suggestion to do what is legitimate in an illegitimate way, i.e. to get what is good in a bad way and to do what is right in a wrong manner it is temptation from the devil.

THE DEVIL'S METHODS

The second temptation which the lord faced shows how far the devil can go in tempting us. "Then the devil taketh him up into the holy city, and setteth him on a pinnacle of the temple, And saith unto him, if thou be the Son of God, cast thyself down: for it is written, He shall give his angels charge concerning thee: and in their hands they shall bear thee up, lest at any time thou dash thy foot against a stone" (Matthew 4:5-6). The devil is subtle. He quoted a scripture in order to lure Jesus into evil. Although the Bible is full of promises on the believer's protection, prosperity and provision, yet they are not to be used wrongfully. The promises of God are meant to relieve the suffering, succour the troubled and provide help for all those in need of divine assistance and miracle.

They are, however, not meant to fulfil our lust or pride. The devil wanted Jesus to take the power of God for granted. He wanted Him to parade His privilege in a vainglorious manner.
Remember that whenever the devil is trying to influence you to do a wrong thing, he will generally quote scriptures in order to convince you. But he often changes, modifies or twists the scriptures or its meaning in order to entice you. That is the strategy of the devil. You must be on your guard at all times lest the devil lures you into evil with his subtlety.

The devil uses a thousand and one methods in seducing people to do what is contrary to the word of God. As if his previous attempt to make the Lord act contrary to the will of God were not enough, Satan came up with another temptation. "Again, the devil taketh him up into an exceeding high mountain, and sheweth him all the kingdoms of the world, and the glory of them; And saith unto him, all these things will I give thee, if thou wilt fall down and worship me" (Matthew 4:8, 9). The things which the devil showed Jesus were not strange to Him. The Lord, obviously, knew that heaven and earth belong to Him. He knew that, at the end of time, there will be a new heaven and a new earth and that as the King of kings and the Lord of lords he will reign over all the earth. Since He is a Divine Personality, he knew that a time was coming when it shall be said that "The kingdoms of this world are become the kingdoms of our Lord, and of his Christ; and he shall reign for ever and ever" (Revelation 11: 15). He also knew that "Of the increase of his government and peace there shall be no end, upon the throne of David, and upon his kingdom, to order it, and to establish It with judgement and with justice" (Isaiah 9:7).

However, He did not yield to the devil's subtle attempt to lure him into seeking for honour and glory outside the will of God. The devil wanted Jesus to take a short cut to his God-appointed destination. It is possible that the Lord has promised you wonderful thing. You must watch it lest Satan, the tempter, succeeds in luring you into making a shipwreck of God's plan for your life. Whatever good thing the Lord has promised you concerning marriage, prosperity and promotion, you must be cautious lest the devil deceive you by showing you wrong ways of possessing your possessions. Do not allow the devil to lure you into compromise, sin and any form of evil. The devil is cunning. He can even use seemingly harmless things to damn your soul. Beware that one of the twelve disciples, was tempted by the devil. Judas opened his heart and his ears to the influence of the tempter. "And supper being ended; the devil having now put into the heart of Judas Iscariot, Simon's son, to betray him" (John 13:2). The devil deceived Judas and convinced him to agree to betray his Lord. The devil lured Judas into selling his soul for thirty pieces of silver. The devil must have really blinded him to make him go into such a damnable and dastardly act. Judas paid dearly for it. He lost his reward, he died a shameful death and he passed into Christless eternity. His eyes became open as soon as he was done with betraying his Lord. But he discovered that it was too late to undo the evil he had done. Do not take the devil or temptations for granted. If you give the devil an inch, he will go a mile. If you give him a chance in your life, he will ruin you eternally. Beware of the first gambits of sin. No matter how little the temptation is, do not give in to the devil (Satan) because if you yield to temptation, you have sinned. The Satan is the main source of temptation. He is the tempter. The following verses clearly explained (1Corinthains.7:5) says "and come together again, that Satan tempt you not for your incontinency….." and (Matthew. 4:1) also says "then was Jesus up led of the spirit into the wilderness to be tempted of the devil". The Bible makes this very clear in (Revelation 12: 9) "And the great dragon was cast out, that old serpent, called the Devil, and Satan, which deceiveth the whole world: he was cast out into the earth, and his angels were cast out with him". The devil, the arch enemy of the children of God, is the brain behind all temptations. He is the one who has lured millions of people into hell. He is also the one who has through temptations, made many believers to go back into the world.

If you yield to Satan's voice you will be cast into the lake of fire. Do not allow the devil to pull you away from the path of righteousness. Having put your hand on the plough, make up your mind to reject the offers of the enemy.

A CALL TO WATCHFULNESS

Having known the source of evil, you are supposed to be on your guard against subtle temptations and all forms of enticement to do what is evil. Besides being watchful and careful at all times not enters into temptation, it is also important that, every believer gets the strength to overcome temptation. The moment we get saved we must be on our guard. The devil can tempt anyone, anytime, anywhere with anything. Jesus said." Watch ye and pray, lest ye enter into temptation" (Mark 14.38). But we must realize that the Lord is our strength in temptation. If you want to overcome temptation, if you need strength to overcome the various temptations that come your way day by day, if you are in need of support and strengths at the time of temptation you need to understand that all the help you need reside in the Lord Jesus Christ. We are told in (Hebrews 2: 17- 18) "Wherefore in all things it behoved him to be made like unto his brethren, that he might be a merciful and faithful high priest in things pertaining to God, to make reconciliation for the sins of the people. For in that he himself hath suffered being tempted, he is able to succour them that are tempted."

OUR STRENGTH IN TEMPTATION

Our strength in temptation is the Lord Jesus Christ himself. Although he was tempted before, but he overcame. The Bible tells us in (Hebrews 2:18) that, "For in that he himself hath suffered being tempted, he is able to succour them that are tempted". Since he himself has been tempted before, he knows the strategy, the methods, and the plans of the devil as well as the baits that the devil normally uses to lure believers into doing his bidding. Being a loving and a compassionate Saviour, the Lord is always ready to succour those who are tempted. Moreover, (Hebrews 4:14-16) says "seeing then that we have a great high priest that is passed into the heavens, Jesus the Son of God; let us hold fast our profession. For we have not an high priest which cannot be touched with the feeling of our infirmities; but was in all points tempted like as we are, yet without sin. Let us therefore come boldly unto the throne of grace that we may obtain mercy, and find grace to help in time of need". The time of temptation is the time of need. The word of God says that you need divine help at the time of temptation. The word of God also makes it clear that Jesus Christ is that divine help. He is the high priest who is touched by the feelings of your infirmities. Jesus does not watch you from a great distance, trying to condemn you during your hour of temptation; rather he is your very present help at the time of temptation. He cares for us — "The Lord Knoweth how to deliver the godly out of temptation, and to reserve the unjust unto the day of judgement" (2 Peter 2:9). This should be an encouragement to children of God. Every believer can bask in the knowledge of the Lord's ability to deliver him from temptations. The Lord is not a novice as far as delivering the godly from temptation. Believers who spend their lives fearing the devil should relax and rejoice in the Lord because, no matter how sorely the devil vexes their souls, the Lord will deliver them. The captain of our salvation has enough ability, power and knowledge. He knows how to deliver the godly out of temptation. Some believers are more conscious of the wicked devices, the strategies and the enticements of the wicked more than the keeping power of God. Some are even defeated before the day of battle. Such people do not really know that "…..greater is He who is in them than he who is in the world" (1 John 4:4). People who are more conscious of the source of temptation may find it difficult to overcome temptation. Believers who often tell stories of those who have fallen prey to the tempter and never talk about God's keeping power and those who have been kept victoriously, may one day become victims to the enemy. If you really believe and always read the Bible you will be more conscious of the supremacy of the great.

One who lives in you over the one who lives in the world and a person who is conscious of the believer's strength in temptation will be quick to make use of it. The fact that the believer must not remain a victim in the hands of the enemy and that he should always overcome temptation cannot be made clearer than in (1Corinthians 10: 13) "There hath no temptation taken you but such as is common to man: but God is faithful, who will not suffer you to be tempted above that ye are able; but will with the temptation also make a way to escape, that ye may be able to bear it". No one can afford to say that his temptations are stronger than the strength of the Lord. None can say that his temptations are above the Lord's control. I want you to know that what you are going through in your office or at home is not without the knowledge of the Lord. He will surely give you the strength to bear your temptation. As a Christian woman, you can be victorious over every temptation. There is no reason why you should yield to temptation. If you ever fall victim to the enemy's trap it will not be because the Lord did not succour you; it will be because you failed to make use of the armour of the Lord. If you are a businessman, you do not have any reason to say that the temptations of the business world are greater than what you can cope with.

Whatever is your profession, you can be victorious if you choose to make use of the strength of the Lord.

REASON FOR BELIEVERS DEFEAT

Those who excuse their sins on the ground that they were sorely tempted do not know the scriptures. The Bible says "Jesus answered and said unto them, Ye do err, not knowing the scriptures, nor the power of God" (Matthew 22:29). When a man and a woman begin to say that they committed sin because their temptation was so strong, they are revealing great ignorance, as far as the revealed will of God is concerned. None can make use of divine strength and yet tell tales of defeat. Generally, those who find it difficult to overcome temptation are those who choose to yield to the devil rather than put on the whole armour of God. If your life has been tarnished by defeat and failure, you ought to examine yourself and seek how to put on the strength of the Lord. A man who is constantly defeated every time he is tempted by the devil: stands-in danger of missing heaven. Heaven is not tor defeated folks; .only overcomers will make heaven. If you want to escape hell, you need to make up your mind to be an overcomer. You can be victorious even if all those around you are yielding to temptations. Although these are perilous time and the devil is fighting his last battle against the souls of men, yet you can remain a victor amidst myriads of ungodly men who drink iniquity like water. It is possible that- you have followed the Lord for a number of years now and you are wondering whether you will be able to make heaven at last.

Do not be troubled. The Lord knows that you will be tempted, but more than that, He knows that His grace is sufficient for you. God has enough power to sustain you and keep you from falling. Remember that, the Lord is able. The strength of the Lord is ever ready for you to ask for. If you lean on the arms of the Lord He will see you through. Lean on the everlasting arms of the Lord and continue to look unto the author and finisher of your salvation, "Now unto him that is able to keep you from falling, and to present you faultless before the presence of his glory with exceeding joy ..." (Jude: 24-25).

STEPS TO VICTORY

Although the Lord is willing to grant you grace at the time of temptation, there are some steps you must personally take in order to experience victory. Whichever way you look at it we all take steps either towards spiritual progress or backsliding.

If the devil succeeds at deceiving you and you yield to temptation, you are taking steps towards backsliding and sin. If you yield on one occasion, he will come against you with a stronger force when he comes to tempt you again.
If you yield to temptation the second time, the devil will look for more avenues for tempting you. He will increase his efforts and he might even work overtime on you. If you keep on yielding to Satan you will eventually become his slave.

On the other hand, if you take positive steps towards overcoming temptation, you will emerge victorious. If the devil tempts you once and you overcome, if he tempts you the second time and you overcome again and if you always overcome each time you are tempted, you are not just trying to be an overcomer you are "more than a conqueror". Bible Christians who walk on the highway of holiness are expected to take certain steps in order to be triumphant over temptation.
Subtle are the devils strategies, if you take the following steps you cannot be anything less than an overcomer. In the economy of grace and in the wisdom of God, the way to triumph over temptation has been made wonderfully simple. Young converts, old believers, adults, teenagers, so- called weak believers as well as Christian workers can make use of proven steps to triumph as contained in the Bible. The steps I am going to show you now can be taken, by everybody. No matter what you have had in the experienced passed and No matter what you are going through right now, if you will diligently carry out these instructions, you shall never fall. The steps are as follows:

RUN FROM EVIL

What then are the steps to triumph? You ask. The answer is One: — Run from evil. We were told in (Proverbs 22:3) "A prudent man foreseeth the evil, and hideth himself but the simple pass on, and are punished". When a prudent believer foresees evil he either hides himself or runs for safety. It is folly to foresee evil in a particular direction and go towards the direction. For example, if you were a drunkard before you will still have to do all you can to keep a distance from your old companions as well as from hotels. If you had problems with prostitutes when you were an unbeliever you will also need to steer clear from the direction of brothels. There are times when you have to run in order to overcome. At times, you will have to change your course and take another direction in order to avoid evil.

You must run away from every appearance of evil. This assertion is enshrined in (Proverbs 4: 14) "Enter not into the path of the wicked, and go not in the way of evil men". If you are a Christian sister, the Lord expects you to keep a distance from your former boyfriends. If you are born again and you want to keep the victory you must watch your movement. Do not enter the path of the wicked. If an old boyfriend comes across your way and offers to render some help, do not consent; it is the devil's strategy for enticing you into evil again. Run. You can avoid the devil and all his traps by using your two legs.

RESIST THE DEVIL

Two, resist the devil. You need to resist the devil if you want to experience victory. The devil will always want to make efforts to destroy you, it is however your duty to resist him. Someone said: "You cannot prevent a bird from flying above you but you can prevent it from making a nest on your head". The Bible also says "Submit yourselves therefore to God. Resist the devil, and he will flee from you" (James 4:7). The devil will flee if you resist him. Whenever the devil tempts you, do not just fold your arms idly, resist him. For instance, if you are being chased by a dog and you keep running in order to avoid being bitten by the dog, it might catch up with you and bite you. On the other hand, if instead of just running away from the dog, you turn around and you shout to scare the dog it might turn back to flee from you. A man once told me about someone who was pursued by a dreadful dog. He ran as fast as he could but the more he ran the closer the dog got to his heels. All of a sudden it dawned on him that, if he did not do something to stop the dog from pursuing him the dog might jump at him and tear him down. He therefore decided to do something about the situation. So, all of a sudden while he was running, he jumped up, turned around and shouted with a loud voice. The dog became afraid and it ran back. That is how to treat the devil. Don't just keep funning, turn around and shout at the devil in the name of Jesus and he will flee from you. Therefore believers should "Be sober, be vigilant; because your adversary the devil, as a roaring lion, walketh about, seeking whom he may devour: Whom resist steadfast in the faith, knowing that the same afflictions are accomplished in your brethren that are in the world" (I Peter 5:8-9).

RENOUNCE SATAN

The third step is to Renounce Satan. Often times, a lot of people fail at the hour of temptation because they have a link with the enemy. Although you are now born again, you need to unembellished every link with Satan. Brethren, consider this statement:— If you have another man's property in your apartment, you would be obliged to allow him in whenever he is at the door or your threshed hold for its collection. This is because there is a link between you and the property's owner (the man in questioned). In the same vein, the devil will always want to come back to you if you are harbouring some of his properties. Charms, Occultism materials, amulets, talisman and all other mundane things belonging to the devil must not be in your custody. If you keep the devil's property, you are building a bridge for the devil to walk over to you. If you want to be an overcomer, all properties of the enemy must be destroyed. Please! Renounce the devil and all his associations with you. The Bible says: "Neither shalt thou bring an abomination into thine house, lest thou be a cursed thing like it: but thou shalt utterly detest it, and thou shalt utterly abhor it; for it is a cursed thing" (Deuteronomy 7:26). This Bible injunction was obeyed by those who came to the Lord Jesus Christ in the early Church. "Many of them also which used curious arts brought their books together, and burned them before all men: and they counted the price of them, and found it fifty thousand pieces of silver" (Acts. 19: 19).

CONFISCATE All STUMBLING BLOCKS / IMPEDIMENTS ON YOUR WAY

The step four is that every believer should remove all stumbling blocks, impediments and hurdles in his /her Christian life. Many people are tempted because they permit stumbling blocks to stand in their ways. If you permit stumbling blocks to remain in your way, either by omission or commission, they will be used by the devil to make you fall. A new convert who still entertains dialogue with former sin partners might go back to his vomit if care is not taken. If you were bound by alcoholism before you became converted, it would be unwise if you still keep some bottles of beer in the house. There are those who say that they do not drink but that they only keep alcohol in the house for entertaining visitors. It is not only sinful to do that, you might one day fall victim to the devil and you will be lured into alcoholism again. But if you make a clean break with the past as soon as you get converted, the devil will find it difficult to lure you into your former sinful habits again. What does the Bible say about stumbling blocks? “And if thy right eye offends thee, pluck it out, and cast it from thee: for it is profitable for thee that one of thy members should perish, and not that thy whole body should be cast into hell. And if thy right hand offend thee, cut it off, and cast it from thee: for it is profitable for thee that one of thy members should perish, and not that thy whole body should be cast into hell” (Matthew 5: 29-30)

CHIDE THE TEMPTER

The fifth step is to reprove the tempter or the temptress. Although the devil is the real tempter, he also uses men and women as agents of temptation (Elements of darkness). Tempters and temptresses should not be viewed as innocent people. If we laugh with every tempter or temptress we are treading dangerous: grounds. “The north wind driveth way rain: so doth, an angry countenance a backbiting tongues” (Proverbs 25:23). When ungodly men and women come to you to tempt you, you must put up an angry countenance. Let them know that you do not joke with sin. Let them, know that you are angry with them. Reprove tempters, and temptresses, do not try to be courteous when sinners try to pull you into sin. If you: want to experience victory in your Christian life, you cannot afford to please everybody. You must be ready to reprove workers of iniquity no matter how/who they are. Peter was a disciple of the Lord Jesus but when he allowed himself to be used by the devil, the Lord Jesus rebuked him sharply. “But when he had turned about and looked on his disciples, He rebuked Peter, saying, Get thee behind me, Satan: for thou savourest not the things that be of God but the things that be of men” (Mark 8:33). There are times when people are not just facing mild temptations from tempters, but they are being tempted by' seducers and Seductresses. When a lady who is possessed by a seducing spirit comes your way, reprove her and keep her at arm’s length. It does not matter who she is, she might either be your superior or she might even be a “respectable” member of the church, you must rebuke her sharply if you want to keep the victory. Let us have some example from the Bible. “And it came to pass after these things that his master's wife cast her eyes upon Joseph; and she said; Lie with me. But he refused, and said unto his master’s wife, Behold my master wotteth not what is with me in the house, and he hath committed all that he hath to my hand; There is none greater in this house than I; neither hath he kept back anything from me but thee, because thou art his wife: how then can I do this great wickedness; and sin against God? And it came to pass, as she spake to Joseph day by day that he hearkened not unto her, to lie by her, or, to be with her. And it came to pass about this time that Joseph went into the house to do his business; and there-was none of the men of the house there within. And she caught him by his garment, saying, lie with me: and he left his garment in her hand, and fled, and got him out. And it came to pass, when she saw that he had left his garment in her hand, and was fled forth” (Genesis 39:7-13). Potiphar’s wife cut the image of a seducer who is bent on achieving her goals. She did not even yield to Joseph’s scathing reprove. She wanted to have Joseph commit immorality with her by all means. After discovering that Joseph would not yield to her enticements, she decided to force him into sin. Joseph did not only reprove her, he took every necessary step in order to experience victory.

He fled from the seductress of a woman in order to keep pure. If you were in Joseph’s shoes what would you have done? If a lady comes to you trying to pull you into sin, you should rebuke her sharply. You must be conscious of the fact that Satan is the brain behind her strange behaviours. Do not try to reason with her. Do not even try to explain why her demands are unreasonable. Rebuke her. If you have to shout at her in order to rebuke her, please do. When a woman comes to you, saying dirty things to you, and you keep quiet, she will want to go further in her efforts to seduce you.

Furthermore, treat a seductress the way you will treat Satan. Rebuke her, shout at her, disgrace her and do everything that will make her know that you cannot joke with sin. On the other hand, if you are a Christian lady and a seducer comes to you, you must show him with your voice as well as with your countenance that you are very angry with him. A lot of men and women have fallen because they treated tempters and temptresses with levity. You must be firm and serious when dealing with agents of the devil.

CULL UNHOLY/ UNCLEANLINESS/ UNRIGHTEOUS THOUGHTS

The sixth step is that; reject the unholy, uncleanliness/ unrighteous thoughts that come on your way. You must reject unholy thoughts whenever they come into your heart. Young believers often have problems with evil thoughts. They say: “I don't know what to do with evil thoughts. I have tried to reject them but the thoughts have remained in my heart. What can I do to overcome the evil thoughts which plague my heart? Brethren when you continue behaving this way, it is like as if you want to fill a big container of water with sand but you are considering how it will get done. However, you need to realise that, it is an easy task. Wise men will tell you that you do not need to burn up your energy by first trying to empty the container before filling it with sand. They will simply tell you to start to pour sand into the filled container and that the more sand you pour into the container the less water will remain in the container. Whenever evil thoughts come into your heart, you only need to feed your heart with the word of God.

As you meditate on God’s word, you will discover that unholy thoughts will begin to disappear as holy thoughts occupy your heart. That is how to get rid of unholy thoughts. The Bible tells us that, “Finally, brethren, whatsoever things are true, whatsoever things are honest, whatsoever things are just, whatsoever things are pure, whatsoever things are lovely, whatsoever things are of good report; if there be any virtue, and if there be any praise, think on these things” (Philippians 4:8).

CONTINUOUSLY REMEMBER THE JUDGEMENT DAY

Seventh step is to remember the judgement day always. If all who are tempted remember the day of judgement at the time of temptation, they will not easily succumb to the enemy’s pressures. This reminds me of what took place many years ago when I was a pupil. Our teachers did not just give us our results privately. They usually summoned our parents and almost everybody in the town usually comes to witness the momentous occasion. The occasion was usually a day of glory for those who did well while it was a moment of shame for those who failed. Whenever I remembered that the whole town would gather together to hear about my performance during the examination, I usually settled down to study earnestly. It would be very helpful to you if you remember judgement day each time you are tempted. Judgement is coming. “And I saw a great white throne, and him that sat on it, from whose face the earth and the heaven fled away; and there was found no place for them. And I saw the dead, small and great, stand before God; and the books were opened, and another book was opened, which is the book of life: and the dead were judged out of those things which were written in the book, according to their works. And the sea gave up the dead which were in it; and death and hell delivered up the dead which were in them: and they were judged every man according to their works. And death and hell were cast into the lake of fire. This is the second death. And whosoever was not found written in the book of life was cast into the lake of fire” (Revelation 20: 11-15)

RELY ON GOD’s PROMISES

The eighth step is to rely on God’s promises. We need to rely on promises of God to overcome temptation. Victory cannot be attainable by leaning on the arms of the flesh. The unfailing promises of God will usher you into victory if you rely on them. “For the hath said, I will never leave thee, nor forsake thee. So that we may boldly say, The Lord is my helper, and I will not fear what man shall do unto me” (Hebrews 13:5-6).

DECLAIM HIS WORD

Ninth step is to recite His word. The Bible makes it clear that the word of God is an invaluable weapon for conquering the enemy. How did the Lord conquer the devil? He conquered the devil by reciting the word of God. When the devil came to tempt the Lord, He recited the word of God saying *“it is written”* each time the devil came. If you cultivate the edifying habit of reciting the word of God, you will always experience victory. Whenever the devil comes to you, talk back to him and stand upon the word, and you will experience resounding victory. Besides, in Joshua God said to him and his people “This book of law shall not depart out of thy mouth; but thou shalt meditate therein day and night, that thou mayest observe to do according to all that is written therein; for then thou shalt make thy way prosperous, and then thou shalt have good success” (Joshua 1:8). One cannot over looked the numerous nitty-gritties found in learning God’s word.

RECEIVE GUIDANCE AND COUNSELLING

The tenth step is to receive counselling. God has raised up pastors and ministers for the edification of the church. You cannot rely on your own wisdom for overcoming temptation. And there are areas of temptations in which you need to be counselled on by your spiritual leaders. If you have tried to overcome the devil without succeeding, try the counselling of God-appointed ministers and leaders. The Bible say "Where no counsel is, the people fall: but in the multitude of counsellors there is safety" (Proverbs, 11: 14).

PATCH-UP THE BROKEN HEDGE

The Eleventh step is to repair the broken hedge. The Bible teaches that there is a hedge around every child of God. However, the hedge can be broken if we allow sin to have an inroad into our lives. Satan recognised the fact that a hedge was built around Job. "Hast not thou made an hedge about him, and about his house, and about all that he hath on every side? Thou hast blessed the work of his hands and his substance is increased in the land" (Job 1: 10). You must ensure that God's hedge around you is always intact lest the evil one infiltrates into your life. "....Whoso breaketh an hedge, the serpent shall bite him" (Ecclesiastes 10: 8). If there is any loophole in your life, do not deceive yourself, repair the broken hedge and the tempter will not be victorious over you. Accept faults and asked for forgiveness always for the Bible says; "He that covereth his sins shall not proper: but whoso confesseth and foraketh them shall have mercy" (proverbs 28:13)

RENEW YOUR HALLOWING

Twelfth step is to, renew your consecration. You need to consecrate your life to the Lord daily. Those who are really committed to the Lord generally experience victory when they are tempted. The Bible says "Neither yield ye your members as instruments of unrighteousness unto sin: but yield yourselves unto God, as those that are alive from the dead, and your members as instruments of righteousness unto God. Know ye not that to whom ye yield yourselves servants to obey, his servants ye are to whom ye obey; whether of sin unto death, or of obedience unto righteousness?" (Romans 6: 13, 16). However you should not depend on the consecrations of yesteryears to grant you victory at the time of temptation. You must renew your consecration daily. In fact, you must consecrate your life to the Lord when you wake up every day. Your spiritual strength will always remain fresh if you cultivate the habit of renewing your consecration daily. If you carry out all these steps diligently, victory will be yours all the days of your life. Instead of regretting in your Christian life, you will always rejoice because of the victory which you will experience. If you take all these steps, you will discover the path to victory and you will be an overcomer.

Finally, remember, it is only overcomers that have been given the promises of abiding and living forever with the Lord. "He that overcometh shall inherit all things, and I will be his God, and he shall be my son" (Revelation 21:7).

Part 3
How to Overcome the Devil

Introduction

The Bible says;"He that hath an ear, let him hear what the Spirit saith unto the churches; To him that overcometh will I give to eat of the tree of life, which is in the midst of the paradise of God. He that hath an ear, let him hear what the Spirit saith unto the churches; He that overcometh shall not be hurt of the second death. He that hath an ear, let him hear what to the Spirit saith unto the churches; To him that over-cometh will I give to eat of the hidden manna, and will give him a white stone, and in the stone a new name written, which no man knoweth saving he that receiveth it. But that which ye have already hold fast till I come. And he that overcometh, and keepeth my work unto the end, to him will I give power over the nations" (Revelation 2: 7, 11, 17, 25, & 26). "He that overcometh, the same shall be clothed in white raiment; and I will not blot out his name out of the book of life, but I will confess his name before my Father, and before his angels. I know thy works: behold, I have set before thee an open door, and no man can shut it: for thou hast a little strength, and hast kept my word, and hast not denied my name. To him that overcometh will I grant to sit with me in my throne, even as I also overcame, and am set down with my Father in his throne" (Revelation 3: 5, 8, & 21).

THE CHALLENGE

In this chapter, we are considering a very serious subject which is very important as far as victorious Christian living is concerned. This may not be the first book you are reading in your Christian life. Perhaps you have read a lot of books by various authors. But as you continue to read this book I want you to approach it with earnestness and directness as it is capable of doing wonderful things in your life. A number of things have led me to write a book like this. Since my coming to Pentecost Church — Ghana; has come a long way and from the first day I started till date, a lot of things have happened to a lot of people. No matter what your own church background is, I am sure your church must have come a long way too. Perhaps, you have also witnessed a number of things in your pilgrim journey, too.

The Christian life is delicate and fragile, and there is a dire need for caution as we fight the battles of life.

If you could recall some believers or Christian workers who were once fiery but are now no longer in the faith, you will be moved with tears. Yes, a lot of people have fallen by the way side. Some people with whom you started the race are no longer following the Lord. Brethren who were once dynamic in faith are wondering whether they are still in the faith or not. Even Christian leaders are not left out; they are also falling. How is the mighty falling! Why are the churches recording so many casualties in the fiery war with the devil? Is the grace of God so inadequate that, the church is recording such appalling incidents of defeat as we hear about? I am depressed whenever I remember those whom I knew when I joined this church aforementioned but are no longer in Christ. Surprisingly! What quite members of the choir, full time-workers, pastors and leaders who once said "We will remain in Christ and in the ministry come what may" but are now backslidden. There are people who were once Bible study leaders, pastors, preachers, counsellors, chorus leaders, ushers and workers in various sections of the ministry but are either no longer in the Kingdom or have had their spiritual lives paralysed. When I looked at all these people and I discovered that they failed because they did not know how to overcome the devil, I decided to provide every believer with sound teaching on how to overcome the devil.

I do not want you to read this book like just like any book — Never. The contents of this book are not to be dallied will victory over the devil is a matter of life and death. It is not what "we" can joke about. I am not trying to discourage you brethren. But I want to tell you that, there are people who were told to watch over their lives lest they fall but felt that they were too strong to experience defeat, Not too soon have such people been warned than they experienced shameful and abysmal death. I called a JSS student and tried to talk to-him on the need to remain steadfast in the Lord. She just stood up and said: "I know that I belong to the Lord, and I am going to remain with the Lord forever". She did not take what I told her seriously and sooner or than later she passed away with serious "Soroku" funeral rites. Admittedly, Judas Iscariot was a disciple of the Lord Jesus Christ, but He did not know that the devil was busy planning to make a shipwreck of his faith. He was ignorant of the strategies of the devil, which lead him fell and lost his minister and apostleship.

FIG – TREE RELIGION

Your present-day position stance in the church does not matter; what matters is your being able to overcome the devil. I do not want to deceive anybody. I know that religion withal victory is vanity. A lot of people are satisfied with "fig - tree religion". Many so-called Christians have settled for a Christian life that knows no victory. I am not like the number of preachers who give God's people sham instead of reality; I am just for the truth. There are believers who do not care about knowing how to overcome the devil. Such believers are satisfied with religion. Concerning them, the scripture aptly says "Having a form of godliness, but denying the power thereof" (2 Timothy 3:5). It is of no use talking about Christianity if there is no victory. There are preachers and writers who never tell God's people about the possibility of victory. You can listen to all their sermons and read all their books without coming across a mentioned of the believer's victorious life. Rather than showing the believer how to overcome the devil, such preachers and writers tell the believer that no one can overcome the devil.

It seems that present day believers are not really interested in knowing how to overcome sin, self and Satan. The Bible says "For the time will come when they will not endure sound doctrine; but after their own lusts shall they heap to themselves teachers, having itching ears; And they shall turn away their ears from the truth, and shall be turned unto fables" (2 Timothy 4:3, 4). Modern day Christians are no longer thirsting for the truth; they are now looking for teachers who will preach according to their tastes. That is why it is becoming increasingly difficult to find real victorious believers in churches, ministries and Christian fellowships. The psalmist foresaw this situation long ago. He prayed "Help, Lord; for the godly man ceaseth; for the faithful fail from among the children of men" (Psalm 12: 1). It seems that, earnestness, faithfulness, victory and spiritual vitality have now become a thing of the past. The watchfulness, the carefulness and the sobriety of the good old days are becoming increasingly difficult to come by.

Modernity is affecting the believer's faith at an alarming rate. The church is becoming worldly and powerless at a very fast pace. Believers are now living as if the devil has already been bound for a thousand years. Many are now becoming careless in spiritual things. It seems we have forgotten the words of the song writer:

Christian seek not yet repose
Cast thy dream of ease away
Thou art in the midst of foes:
"Watch and pray"
Principalities and powers,
Mustering their unseen array,

Wait for thy unguarded hours
"Watch and pray"

Gird thy heavenly armour on,
Wear it every night and day;
Ambushed lies the Evil One;
"Watch and pray"

Hear the victors who overcame;
Still thy mark each warrior's way;
All with one sweet voice exclaim
"Watch and pray".

It seems we have also forgotten the words of the Lord Jesus. "And take heed to yourselves, lest at any time your hearts be overcharged with surfeiting, and drunkenness, and cares of this life, and so that day come upon you unawares. For as a snare shall it come on all them that dwell on the face of the whole earth. Watch ye therefore, and pray always, that ye may be accounted worthy to escape all these things that shall come to pass, and to stand before the Son of man" (Luke 21:34-36). May God open your eyes to the need for watchfulness as you read this book (Amen).

THE DEVIL'S STRATEGY

In Revelation 3:21, Jesus says "To him that overcometh will I grant to sit with me in my throne, even as I also overcame, and am set down with my Father in his throne". The sins besetting believers today, the suggestions of the enemy, the temptations of the devil, the arrows of Satan, the fiery darts from the wicked one, the tricks of the believer's arch-enemy and the suggestions of the adversary are so much that the believer needs to muster all his spiritual strength in order to remain victorious. The devil wages war against believer every moment and he uses all kinds of strategy in order to make the believer fall. Often times, he aims at making the believer to turn back from following the Lord by hauling fiery temptations at him/her. He also uses discouragement as a weapon in order to make the Christian pilgrim weary of following the Lord. Also, he tries to instil fear into the heart of the believer in order to make him dread taking steps of obedience and faith. In all, the methods deployed by the devil are aimed at luring the believer away from the path of righteousness. Jesus knows that, it is possible to remain victorious in the midst of ravaging attacks from the devil. He knows that, even if the majority are choosing defeat, there are some people who are going to overcome the devil. By virtue of the fact that, you belong to Christ, you are supposed to be victorious all the days of your life. As a child of God, you are not supposed to dread the devil, rather you are supposed to make him tremble and flee whenever he tries to come against you as Jesus was victorious when he once lived on this world, so should every earnest believer be victorious. The arrows of the devil, the fiery darts of the accuser of the brethren, and the devices of the wicked one were all hauled at the Lord Jesus when He was here on earth, but He overcame. He has promised that He will make all who will eventually overcome to sit with Him on His throne.

Furthermore, Temptations will come whether you like it or not brethren. Whether you are hiding or exposing yourself, temptation will come. If you are always alert and watchful, you will not be taken by surprise when the enemy comes. You must be prepared at all times to face the enemy's attack. When you are prepared, you will find it easy to face the enemy and overcome him whenever he comes against you.

THE BELIEVERS' VICTORS AND VICTIMS

Although the devil tries to wage war against all believers yet there are a group of believers who always overcome Right from the Bible days, people have either been victors or victims. Some people have had a testimony of victory and dominion while some others have fallen on the battlefield. Although Enoch was tempted, yet he had a testimony of victory. The devil launched an attack on Joseph by tempting him with immorality; yet he was victorious. But the same bait was used by Satan against David; he fell victim to the enemy's gambit. Samson was a mighty man but he fell when enemy tempted him. On the other hand, Judas Iscariot, and John, the beloved, were all on the same battle field fighting against Satan, and Judas fell in the midst of the battle while John was faithful unto death and qualified for overcomer's crown. There are always two groups of people; those who overcome and those who experience defeat.

We do not overcome the devil because of our religious inducement and neither do we overcome the devil because of the church we belong to. There are Evangelicals, Pentecostals or Charismatics who do not know what it means to overcome the devil. A lot of people who speak in tongues, fast and pray have fallen into the tempter's snare and have experienced defeat. A lot of preachers have fallen because of women and so no and so forth. Many preachers who once had dynamic and anointed ministries have fallen because of money, and others have fallen because of pride or ambition. Those who once overcame the devil are now being overcomers. Hence, you cannot overcome the devil through positive confession. If you don't watch your life well, you will be defeated despite your powerful confessions. Think about those who have been defeated already as a touchstone, and do not allow anybody to deceive you. Note that, victory does not come by chance. It takes diligence, watchfulness, earnestness and seriousness to overcome the devil. There are those who go about confessing that they are overcomers without having been experienced victory over the devil. Many of modern day preachers have failed to tell God's people the truth concerning overcoming the devil that is why many are not experiencing victory. You need to cast aside all man-made strategies and go into the word of God for proven principles of victorious Christian living. How many modern day believers can testify to possess the type of victory that men like Enoch, Joseph, Samuel, John and Paul experienced in the olden days? Do we see much of Bible Christianity around? How many victorious believers do we have in various churches, assemblies and fellowships? Are churches not filled with people who profess victory publicly but cry secretly because sin and Satan have bowed them down?

GOD'S WILL FOR ALL BELIEVERS

God's will is that, the way of victory should be made known to all His children. There are many believers who are desperately searching for the way of victory. They are tired of experiencing defeat, and they want to know what steps to take in order to become overcomer. Right from Bible days, there have been people who have shunned mediocrity and defeat. God has never lacked people who demonstrate the possibility of being victorious. For instance, the three Hebrew children Shadrack, Meshack and Abednego chose victory and protectorate when they found themselves in a strange land. There were thousands of Israelites in Babylon then when king Nebuchadnezzar commanded everyone to bow down to his idol worshiping, but notwithstanding, Shadrack, Meshack and Abednego stood out from the crowd by refusing to follow the multitude to do evil. "....be it known unto thee, O king, that we will not serve thy gods, nor worship the golden image which thou hast setup" (Daniel 3:18). Their action was reported to Nebuchadnezzar. They refused to bow down even after they had sensed the anger and the fury in the heart of king Nebuchadnezzar. They refused to bow down even after they had been told that they will be cast into the midst of burning fiery furnace. Overcomers and victors are those who have made up their minds not to bow before the devil. If you want to get to heaven, you need to make up your mind to overcome whatever it will cost you. Nebuchadnezzar may rage, Pharaoh may threaten, the chariots of Pharaoh may be behind you, and the devil may roar like a hungry lion, all these will not move a man who is determined to make heaven. Shadrack, Meshach and Abednego were not only threatened, they were actually bound and cast into the burning fiery furnace. "And he commended the most mighty men that were in his army to bind Shadrack, Meshach and Abednego, and cast them into the burning fiery furnace"
(Daniel 3:20). They were not shaken neither were they afraid; they kept their testimony. God rewarded their faithfulness by shielding them from being burnt in the fiery furnace.

However, Daniel was also tempted by the enemy but he overcame. If some so-called believers were to be in Daniel's shoes, they would have compromised. Daniel stood alone and he overcame. Also, his life was not only threatened, he was also thrown into the den of lions "....so the king gave order, and they brought Daniel and threw him into the lions' den..." (Daniel 6:16). Daniel lived an overcomer's life. Nobody was watching Daniel whether he was going to stand or not. The temptation came and the threatening was severe but he overcame. I have made up my mind to be an overcomer; and right now, the greatest and the most important thing to me is to have a life that is free from sin. I have decided to live a life that is so spotlessly clean that, if you take a knife and cut my life open, you will not see any dirt or secret thing. I know there are promises of healing in the Bible, and I thank God for many numerous thousands who have been healed and delivered, hence I know that, having my name in the book of life is more important than healing and casting out devils. I know that believers should speak in tongues, and I believe that spiritual gifts are for today's believers but there is nothing valuable than living an overcoming life and holiness I extol above all things. I vehemently believe that, we don't know when Jesus will come and we don't know when the rapture will take place but if we live victorious (overcomer's) lives, we will always be sure of making heaven.

As believers of the gospel, we should always examine our relationship with the God in order to ascertain whether our lives are always acceptable before Him. It is unwise to wait for the time of the rapture in order to check up if your Christian life meets God's standard of righteousness and holiness. Besides, anybody can preach; yes of course! But preachers should be seriously mindful about their choice of massage. Judas and Demas preached yet they went to hell. Who cannot preach? The Pharisees, hypocrites, backsliders and uncovered men and women can preach. It is much easier to preach about victory than to experience the victorious Christian life. The fact that you preach the gospel does not exempt you from fulfilling God's standard of holiness. Only overcomers will reign with Jesus in eternity. If you are alone like Daniel, you need to watch your words, actions and thoughts. If a man/lady knows that you are alone, he/she might come to you in order to lure you into immorality. If you succumb to his/her wishes thinking that, you can get away with it since nobody knows about it, does God don't know it? Even if you try to cover it up, can you cover it up from God? Don't you know that a secret sin on earth is an open scandal in heaven? Will you try to cover your sin with laughter and boldness? Will you hide under the cloak of speaking in tongues? If you were to be alone in Babylon would you have been able to take your stand like Daniel? If Daniel could overcome, you do not have any excuse for not overcoming.

THE TEMPTATIONS OF JESUS

The devil is the arch-enemy of man and he is also the deceiver. He deceives and he tempts. The Bible has revealed how he tempts. The temptation of Jesus was recorded in scripture to enable us understand the devices of the enemy. The temptation of those who were victorious and the temptation of those who were defeated by the devil have all been documented in the Scripture in order to make us learn from their experiences.

- How then does the devil tempt? The devil tempts by exaggerating the needs of people, magnifying their problems, and giving them ungodly suggestions. The devil is so subtle and diabolical that he can offer you seemingly reasonable and helpful advices or help without knowing his real intentions. The devil will advise a man or a boy to try masturbation; telling him "after all, you have not got married". The devil exaggerated Jesus' needs asking Him to turn stones to bread — that was temptation; the devil can exaggerate any need in your life. If you are a student, the devil may exaggerate your academic needs beyond measure in order to take the Bible away from you. Also, the devil may exaggerate your needs in the area of marriage to the point of making you sin against God. He will so exaggerate your needs that you will be thinking of marriage in the morning, noon and night. As soon as he gets you to look at your needs in his perspective he will then go ahead to tempt you.

- How else does the devil tempt? He tempts by presenting people with a twisted picture of God's word and God's will. He specialises in twisting scripture and changing God's word. He often adds to the word of God with the view of luring the innocent man from the path of righteousness. For example, he told Jesus "If thou be the Son of God, cast thyself down: for it is written, He shall give his angels charge concerning thee: and in their hands they shall bear thee up, lest at any time thou dash thy foot against a stone" (Matthew 4:6) in order to make Him sin against God. The devil misquoted Psalm 91 verses eleven and twelve in order to make Jesus tempt God. The devil often changes scripture (adds to it or subtracts from it) as well as misinterprets scripture; misapplies Scripture so as to tempt you and make you do what is contrary to the word of God. Your mother may misquote the Bible in order to make you go against God's will. Your father may misquote the Bible to you saying "After all doesn't the Bible says obey your parents in all things? Your colleagues may also try to lure you into sin by saying "Bribery and corruption is not sinful; doesn't the Bible says that, heaven helps those who help themselves?" You must watch your interactions with people and do not accept everything that people tell you at its face value. Wherever people quote the Bible to you, check-up if it is properly quoted.

- The devil also tries to make believers to fall by exhibiting the glory of the kingdom of the world. That was exactly what the devil did when he took Jesus up into an exceeding high mountain, and "sheweth him all the kingdoms of the world, and the glory of them" (Matthew 4:8). How does the devil do this today? He tempts believers by parading the fashions of this world in an alluring way. He also tempts by projecting the dazzling glories of the kingdom of this world on commercials, in newspapers and magazines and on the television screen, internets etc.. The devil will tempt a Christian lady by showing her ladies that are flashy dressed and decked with jewellery and cosmetics. The devil will tell the Christian lady "See what! You are missing; if you just deny Christ these, other things will be yours". The devil could promise you the vanities of the world and promise you satisfaction and joy. If he knows that, you can easily be lured into sin through fashion, he will use it to draw you. If he knows that, you will easily be diverted from the way of the Lord through the love of money, he will use just that. If he knows that, if he uses women or men, as bait in drawing your soul to hell, he will succeed, he will resort to that wicked device. The devil will show you the things of the world and persuade you like he persuaded Eve saying "Has God said that you should not enjoy anything at all?" (Genesis 3:1). He will show you 'So-called believers' who have liberty to do as they like. He will do all these in order to make you sin against God. The devil will often try to tempt you while you are alone. He tempted Eve while she was alone. The enemy will shoot his arrows at you when you are alone, — evil thoughts and evil suggestions will come into your heart when there is no one around you to act as a check on your spiritual life. That is the strategy of the devil.

SATAN'S DEVICES

Another thing that the devil does in order to make people live defeated lives is that, he removes the word of God from the heart of men and women. The devil always aims at removing God's word from the heart of those who are negligent and careless. The devil tries to remove the word of God from your heart in order to plant doubt, unbelief, and desire for sin there. He tries to remove the promises of God from your heart in order to make you think that you can live an independent life without God. The devil generally attempts to sweep away God's word from people's heart before he sweeps his debris into it. Whenever the devil comes into your heart trying to tamper with God's word, resist him. "Those by the way side are they that hear; then cometh the devil and taketh away the word out of their hearts, lest they should believe and be saved" (Luke 8: 12). If you are so serious with the word of God, the devil will try to bring other interesting things into your heart in order to addle you. If you have been so serious with the word of God on restitution, sanctification and holiness, the devil will persuade you to begin to read books in faith, possibility thinking, healing and prayers. The more you read so called faith books, the more the devil will try to convince you that restitution, sanctification and holiness are not quite necessary. The devil will be telling you that, the most important thing now is speaking in tongues so forget about the aforementioned things, and will persistently coaxed you until losing your conviction. The devil knows that, he could easily overcome you by succeeding in removing God's word from your heart, and so now therefore will do everything possible to remove it from your heart. He will try to make you develop interest in other things at the expense of your commitment to the doctrine of holy living and God. He will allow you to stuff your heart with chaff while trying everything possible to steal away God's word and plant error, deceit and false doctrine there. The devil will bring up insinuating questions in your mind. He will ask you silently but subtly: "Are you the only person going to heaven? Why are you so strict? Is God not a God of mercy? Will God throw you to hell just because you are not able to meet up with His standard? Does God not know that we are all weak?

DECEIT

Do not allow the devil to deceive you into believing that, God will lower his standard or change his word just because of you. The Bible says "Know ye not that the unrighteous shall not inherit the kingdom of God? Be not deceived: neither fornicators, nor idolaters, nor adulterers, nor effeminate nor abusers of themselves with mankind, nor thieves, nor covetous, nor drunkards, nor revilers, nor extortioners, shall inherit the kingdom of God" (1Corinthians 6: 9-10). The devil will want to deceive you, by telling you that you can commit fornication once in a while and still get to heaven if you repent. The devil will do everything possible to convince you that fornication is not an unpardonable sin in order to damn your soul. If you are married, be watchful. The devil will try to deaden your conscience in order to lure you into adultery.

Nevertheless, the devil will never allow a polygamist to understand that having more than one wife or being married to a woman that is not one's first wife is sinful. The devil will coaxed adulterers, liars, drunkards, and homosexuals, and make them believe that they are not too bad. Be watchful at all times. Do not be deceived. The devil is a master strategist. He is a schemer who uses numerous methods in order to make believers stumble and fall on the way to heaven. He tells lies, he deceives and he presents error in a clever way in order to make people sin against God. He sets traps for innocent souls in order to lure them into hell. He terrifies and makes people afraid in order to make them tread the path of ungodliness. He threatens mankind in order to make them victimized to his diabolical plans and intentions. He instigates people to do what is seemingly wrong by making them to lose sight of the consequences of disobedience and sin.

PROVOCATION

One of the major tools Satan uses to deter man from his creator is Provocation. In the Bible, Satan tried this scheme in (1 Chronicles 21:1) "And Satan stood up against Israel, and provoked David to number Israel." The devil knows his goal and he generally does everything in order to deprive him from achieving his goal, and also make him displease God. The devil is still busy provoking people to commit sin; steal, committing immorality, while others to violate God's word even after they have known his words are just and true. If you want to be an overcomer, you must pray at all times against the devices of the devil.

COSTLY NEGLIGENCE

Some years back, a brother told me that, he refuses to listen to preaching topics on anything except faith and evangelism. He said all he wanted to hear from the pulpit were messages on the dynamics of faith, "Go ye ... Preach to every creature", that's all he needed: evangelism massages. He was not interested in listening to messages on holiness, victorious Christian living and preparing for the Lord's coming etc. and was eager to go out and evangelise. Then I looked at him, and told him that, he needed to sit down and get himself saturated with the word of God. I discouraged him from concentrating on evangelism activity alone. I wanted him to build up his spiritual life. He discountenanced my counsels, went out to do what he was not prepared to do. Sooner than later got into trouble and arrested. He lied and started drifting away from God. After that, he started lusting after women. A lot of things happened to him. He came back defeated and backslidden. He came back telling me "I have come to learn. I did not listen in the past. Now I want to listen". But before he realised the importance of listening to sound doctrine, he really suffered. He prayed like Esau. He sobbed and cried profusely all to no avail. He even tried fasting yet he could not find any solution to his predicament. He tried almost everything in order to be restored yet there was no solution. He suffered for months in that terrible state. He ran out of town and went to a remote village. The devil still tempted and tortured him there. Eventually, he had to rise up in a local church saying "Look at me. I am a defeated fellow. If you can pray for a backslider, please pray for me". And the whole church really prayed for him. However, the people's prayer did not bring any change to his situation. One day he decided to go back to what he had neglected. He started reading the word of God. He picked up a tract and he started reading it. During that period things had really gone bad for him (Life was meaningless), food was tasteless. He had no fellowship with man or God, and had a famished soul. He was just running about like a vagabond. But as he was driven back to the Bible, he began to experience a change in his circumstances. As he read the tract, the light of God shone from heaven. He surrendered to God there and then, and he came back restored and revive. It was then he told me that he was ready to listen to anything preached besides evangelical topics.

IT IS WRITTEN

The devil is a tempter. He has defeated many people. But you can overcome him if that is your choice. How do we overcome? Jesus overcomes by the word. He said: *"It is written"*, the first time he was tempted (Matthew 4:6). The devil went away and came back the second time. When the devil came back, Jesus said: *"It is written"* again (Matthew 4:8). The devil went away and came the third time. Jesus used the same weapon. He said: *"It is written"* (Matthew 4:10). Jesus conquered the devil through the word of God. The word of God is the sword of the Spirit (Ephesians 6:16). It is a powerful spiritual weapon which you must make god use of it, if you want to overcome the devil. But if we are not careful, we can get to the point where members spend precious hours other church activities without having enough time to read their Bibles. How can they overcome without making god use of the sword of the Spirit? If they are so committed to the ministry, but do not know their left from the right as far as spiritual warfare is concerned; pity is theirs. What good is the church that is composed of defeated: backslidden and morally weak men and women do to a God's church? It will be sad, if we ever get to a point where we are only concerned about carnality at the expense of Christian living.

CHANGING STANDARDS

The Church is at fast alarming rate becoming worldly, and Christian standard is fast denigrating. I am sure early churches did not start like this. If you listen to the conversation of many Christians of date, what you will hear over and over again are statements about worldly things like getting: Work, Money, Marriages, Naming ceremony but few to mention. Things have changed: Heaven is no more our prime focus. We only give secondary attention to spiritual things now, for notwithstanding the fact that 'Half-hearted believers' cannot overcome. If you are so given to activities to the point of neglecting your spiritual life, you are treading on dangerous grounds. The Bible has warned us about Perilous times to come and the love of the world than loving God. "For men shall be lovers of their own selves, covetous, boasters, proud blasphemers, disobedience to parents, unthankful, unholy, Without natural affection, trucebreakers, false accusers, incontinent, fierce, despisers of those that are good, Traitors, heady, highminded, lovers of pleasures more than lovers of god" (2Timothy 3: 2- 4). Being full of worldly activities without being filled with the mind of Christ leads a soul to hell. If we do not watch our lives, we can go on in activities until we have lost every touch with heaven. We might get to a point where we always think about seminars, evangelism, visitation, outreaches, follow-up and workers meetings and conferences without any consideration for our spiritual lives. If members of the church get to a point when they are always busy planning and carrying out personal evangelism, prison evangelism, village evangelism, hospital evangelism and street evangelism until they no longer have time for their quiet time, the Church is in trouble. Pity and sorrowfulness is ours if we are so full of activities to the point of waking up in the morning for worldly activities without reading your Bible. The devil will be happy if that ever happens. He knows that one can only overcome, if he/she is spiritually alright. He also knows that he can overcome all those who, though are very active, are very weak spiritually.

PERTINENT QUESTIONS

Believers must be very watchful about their personal Christian life, because being very busy at work and never allow yourself to get busy to the point of neglecting your personal Christian life. Some years ago, I was invited to preach to Christian students on campus. I preached a powerful sermon and the people were wonderfully blessed. Something unusual happened after the meeting. A young Christian girl walked up to me and said, Sir, I want to ask you some questions?. Would you answer them? I said Yes; thinking that she came for counselling on some issues in her Christian life. How is your quiet time? was her first surprising question. I said Thank God it is alright. Then she said: How is your prayer life? I told her that my prayer life was alright Then she probed further Sir, do you have any problem in your Christian life? I thank God there is no problem I answered. She looked at me again Are you having enough time for Bible reading and prayer? Are you sure that you are not too busy to the point of becoming empty spiritually? The person who came up with these entire pertinent questions was just a young undergraduate at that time. I thank God for her concern and sincerity. I wonder how many of us are so concerned about our spiritual welfare today.

MISPLACED PRIORITIES

I know that it is possible to be buried in activities until we no longer have time for ourselves. It is quite possible to be so busy to the point of having no time for our families. If there is anything that causes sorrow in my heart, it is believer's ignorance in spiritual things. Do not deceive yourself. Settle all spiritual leniencies. If there is anything that causes sorrow in my heart, is the fact that, many leaders, preachers, and full time Christian workers have no time to read the Bible. They are so busy that their knowledge of God's word is shallow that if they are called upon to preach, they might not know how to rightly share the word of truth. If we are so sound on administration, and if we are so busy with activities but we are weak as far as the knowledge of the word of God is concerned, we will never know what it means to be an overcomer. How can we overcome if we are not familiar with God's word? The word of God is the strength of the believer's life. Regardless of this, the Bible says: "For the word of God is quick, and powerful, and sharper than any twoedged sword, piercing even to the dividing asunder of soul and spirit, and of the joints and marrow, and is a discerner of the thoughts and intents of the heart" (Hebrews 4:12). If we neglect God's word, we are neglecting the backbone of our spiritual lives, and cannot spend quality time with God's word we cannot overcome. Why do we no longer read our Bibles? Some believers only read the Bible at a superficial level. Only very few still find time to dig deeper into God's word, why won't the devil defeat us with fornication and adultery etc. when we are no longer the type of believers we used to be?. Perhaps it may not be long before we shall start hearing of people who profess to be saved, sanctified and baptised in the Holy Ghost divorcing their wives and dealing with all sought of peril because they are no longer committed to the word of God. I prefer that, we cast activities aside and concentrate on how to be overcomers. I know that when Jesus comes at the rapture, He is coming for overcomers, not for those who are addicted to activities. You had better get your Christian life in order before it becomes too late. Remember that if you miss heaven you have missed everything.

The moment we begin to shift our emphasis away from Bible Christianity and we begin to copy the lifestyle of other so-called Christians, of which we have already lost what makes us unique. Do you still understand sanctification? When last did you study God's word on holiness and sanctification Do you still believe that without holiness no man shall see the Lord? The Bible entreat us to "Follow peace with all men, and holiness, without which no man shall see the lord" (Hebrews 12:14). Are you still holy- in body and in spirit? Has the hedge of holiness been broken in your life? Are you not so busy doing the work of the Lord that you do not have time to fellowship with the Lord of the work? Do you still have time for prayer?

How is your spiritual life now? Is it in shambles? Do not hide anything. Be sincere to yourself and be open to God. If you allow the Lord to bring the seriousness of yesteryears back into your life, you will experience the touch of God once again.

TREADING ON DANGEROUS GROUND

The act of treading on dangerous ground leads to perishable soul and for that reason, the Lord is calling you to watchfulness: "And that, knowing the time, that now it is high time to awake out of sleep: for now is our salvation nearer than when we believed; Awake to righteousness, and sin not; for some have not the knowledge of God: I speak his to your shame" (Romans 13: 11; 1 Corinthians 15: 34). You need to watch if you are fond of talking to the point you sin against God. You need to watch if you have the tendency of exaggerating facts, whenever you talk. If you do not watch, the devil will soon defeat you, for the Bible says in (James 3: 2) that, "For in many things we offend all. If any man offend not in word, the same is a perfect man, and able also to bridle the whole body." Are you in the enemy's claws? Have you allow the love of money and the thing of this world to erode your spiritual life? It does not matter what you are called and what office you occupy in the church, the devil will trample upon you if he knows that, you are a hypocrite. Let me tell you this; devil knows true Christians. If you put your hope in positive confession saying 'I am an overcomer'; 'I cannot be defeated', 'the devil cannot overcome me because I am a child of God' without obeying God's word diligently, you cannot be an overcome. If you allow your need for a child, a wife or a job to take the greatest part of your attention from God, you are far from being an overcomer. If you so desire going to school to the point of saying "I don't even care if the devil gives me a scholarship"; I will get it because I am in need of a sponsorship. Even if I compromise, God understands", you are not treading on the path of the overcomer.

SOBERNESS AND WATCHFULNESS

The scripture says: "Be sober, be vigilant; because your adversary the devil as a roaring lion, walketh about, seeking whom he may devour; Whom resist steadfast in the faith, knowing that the same afflictions are accomplished in your brethren that are in the world" (1 Peter 5:8-9). Are we still sober? The bible also warned us that, "Therefore let us not sleep, as do others; but let us watch and be sober" (Thessalonians 5:6) and (1Peter 4:7) also said "But the end of all things is at hand: be bye therefore sober, and watch unto prayer." In James (1:7-8) says: "For let not that man think that he shall receive any thing of the Lord. A double minded man is unstable in all his ways." I do not like to deceive you. I just want to tell you the truth. If you do not live soberly and carefully, you cannot overcome the devil, and therefore have heaven at hand.

RESISTING THE DEVIL

The devil will always try to wage war against you but you can overcome him even if he comes against you a thousand times. If you resist the devil you will be an overcomer. How do I resist the devil? You asked. The Bible says in (James 4:7) that; "Submit yourselves therefore to God. Resist the devil, and he will flee from you." You must resist the devil by rejecting all that he tries to offer you. If the devil offers you a lady, reject her. If he offers you money, reject it. He can come to you with a suggestion, reject his suggestion. Then you must rebuke the devil and exercise your authority over him. Jesus said "Upon this rock I will build my church; and the gates of hell shall not prevail against it" (Matthew 16: 18). Rebuke the devil and claim your victory because it has been prophesied in the word of God. Romans (16:20) says "And the God of peace shall bruise Satan under your feet shortly." Do not accept defeat, and dare to be an overcomer. Take authority over the tempter; when he brings suggestions, and keep them under your feet. If he brings temptation, trample upon it, and above all, stand firmly against Satan and claim your victory. Remember that Christ has given you for victory at Luke (10: 19); "Behold, I give unto you power to tread on serpents and scorpions, and over all the power of the enemy: and nothing shall by any means hurt you." Similarly, He gave us power at Mark (16:17-18), which says; "And these signs shall follow them that believe; in my name shall they cast out devils; they shall speak with new tongues; They shall take up serpent; and if they drink any deadly thing, it shall not hurt them; they shall lay hands on the sick, and they shall recover" as well as Matthew and Mark (10:1; 3:15) respectively. Finally, remember that the Bible says; "Whoever resisteth power, resisteth the ordinance of God: and they that resist shall receive to themselves damnation" (Roman 13:2).

POSSIBILITIES OF VICTORY

Finally we are told in (1 John 5:18) that: "We know that whosoever is born of God sinneth not; but he that is begotten of God Keepeth himself, and that wicked one toucheth him not." These of us who are born again know that, it is possible to overcome the devil. We now that victory is the 'birth-right' of all who are genuinely born again. "We know that whosoever is born of God sinneth not". Those who are born again do not play with sin. They do not experiment with sin; neither do they commit sin moderately. More so, from the above clause "We know that whosoever is born of God sinneth not; but he that is begotten of God keepeth himself" shows that believers are expected to keep themselves from being defeated by the devil. Your victory is in your own hands through the grace of our Lord Jesus Christ that is why he said: "Behold, l gave unto you the power to tread on serpents and scorpions, and over all the power of the enemy: and nothing shall by any means hurt you". If you know you have not been living in victory, there is no point just running ahead. You can decide for victory now, so revenge on the devil for He has defeated you for so long. He has cheated you for so long. Jesus Christ wants to redeem you from the bondage of the devil that why the scripture says; Stand fast therefore in the liberty wherewith Christ hath made us free, and be not entangled again with the yoke of bondage (Galatians 5:1). Besides, Hebrews (2:15) stipulates that "And deliver them who through fear of death were all their lifetime subject to bondage." But, remember, if you give only ninety five per cent of your life to the Lord, He will reject it. If you try to serve the Lord a little and serve the devil a little, you will never be able to make it. Let me remind you of what Jesus said "To him that overcometh will I grant to sit with me in my throne, even as I also overcame, and am set down with my Father in His throne" (Revelation 3:21). The Lord is coming for overcomers. Do not deceive yourself. Settle all things with the Lord today and you will be sure of spending eternity in heaven. One of the ways you could defeat your enemies is to know their strategies, how they operate and the weapons they use. "For we wrestle not against flesh and blood, but against principalities, against powers, against the rulers of the darkness of this world, against spiritual wickedness in high places" (Ephesians 6:12).

About the Author

Bertino Baabereyir Richard, is an ordained Deacon and a member of Pentecost Church of Ghana for over ten years, and has been instrumental in the church activities as well as the Pentecost Student Association (PENSA) activities at the University Level and beyond. By the special grace of God upon his life, the Holy Spirit has used him in diverse ways to establish testimonies in many lives.

He holds a Master of Philosophy in Construction Technology. He is Building Engineer and a Teacher by Profession. He has married to Marfowaa Agyei -Agyemang Ernestina, and their marriage is blessed with a daughter – Irenia Yuor Bertino Baabereyir. The author currently lives in Kumasi-Abuakwa.

First Order Spiritual Decree

Ye malicious intent and evil spirits: ye spirits and agents of darkness and witchcraft; ye agent of Aradia (Prince of wizards); ye Powers of darkness of the realm of Satan, in the Mighty Name of our Lord Jesus Christ, let the Spirit of God Jehovah banish all your plots and schemes against me.

By the second Command of the Holy Spirit, let all your plans and snare against me, and those hovering with me encounter with the blood of Jesus Christ. Above all evil and devilish incarnates, I am free, I am free, I am free, and I am free. I am over witches, wizards, and the powers of dark ages now and forever through the name of our Lord Jesus Christ, so it be. Amen! Amen!! Amen!!!

Second Order Spiritual Decree

In the Most Blessed Name of our Lord Jesus Christ: the Lord of Host and Saviour of the world, and by the strength of the Seven Spirits of God; I vehemently call forth the Spirits of God from the Throne of the Living God Jehovah. Let the Spirit of God invade through my spirit, soul and body, and uproot and banish any element of darkness in me; uproot, destroy, throw abode and banish all that are not instituted in me by the Father in Heaven.

I am that I am with the endless power of God Almighty in motion! Pass through me and banish al that are less below belt than the perfection of Christ; let it be done now, in the Holy Name of my Lord and Personal Saviour Jesus Christ. Amen! Amen!! Amen!!!

Third Order Spiritual Decree

Through the blameless and spotless perfect blood of Jesus Christ, the lord and saviour of the universe; I command you to flee away from my catchment arena, my life, ye Yamadutas (spirits of death).

Let the spirit of fear depart and flee far away from me. Oh! Ye spirits of death let your power and devilish devices against me perish in the great thick smoke fire of the Lord of Host– the Consuming Fire. I am free, I am free, I am free, and I am free, for as long as I live faithfully, truthfully and worthy for the Blessings of the Lord Jesus Christ. Amen! Amen!! Amen!!!

Fourth Order Spiritual Decree

Behold darkness flee before thee, and now let the shadows of seep-waves depart from me and fade pale away. Oh! My Lord, the Omnipotent, you are extremely powerful than thick smoke of fire; You are the Consuming Fire: Consume! Consume!! Consume!!! Every "Sleep- wave" that shall come hereafter against me. Let it be done now by Your Mighty Power, in the name of Jesus Christ. Amen! Amen!! Amen!!!

Amen!

Table of Contents

MIX
Papier aus verantwortungsvollen Quellen
Paper from responsible sources
FSC® C105338

Printed by Books on Demand GmbH, Norderstedt / Germany